Personal Licence Holder's Guide

Scotland: For both On- and Off-licence Premises

Certificate for Scottish Personal Licence Holders
(On Sales) 7104–01

Certificate for Scottish Personal Licence Holders
(Off Sales) 7104–02

First published 2007
Reprinted 2008 (twice), 2009, 2010, 2011

ISBN 978-0-85193-129-6

Cover and book design by Purpose Ltd
Implementation by Max Ackermann
Typeset in Congress Sans
Printed in the UK by Norwich Colour Print

Alcohol Focus Scotland is the Scottish
national charity for alcohol issues. ServeWise
is the training arm of Alcohol Focus Scotland
providing training for people working at all
levels within the licensed trade in Scotland.
All ServeWise courses meet the necessary
legislative requirements.
T   +44 (0)141 572 6700
F   +44 (0)141 333 1606
E   enquiries@alcohol-focus-scotland.org.uk
W   www.alcohol-focus-scotland.org.uk

City & Guilds is the UK's leading provider of
vocational qualifications, offering over 500
awards across a wide range of industries. With
over 8400 centres in 100 countries, City &
Guilds is recognised by employers worldwide
for providing qualifications that offer proof of
the skills they need to get the job done.
W   www.cityandguilds.com

Copies of this book may be obtained from:
    City & Guilds
    1 Giltspur Street
    London EC1A 9DD

For publication enquiries:
T   +44 (0) 844 543 0000
E   learningmaterials@cityandguilds.com

Contents

Introduction

This book is written as a guide for those who are seeking to gain their Certificate for Scottish Personal Licence Holders under the Licensing (Scotland) Act 2005. It covers both on-licence and off-licence premises.

It contains all the required content for the personal licence holders' qualification, plus additional material that may be useful to you in the management of your premises.

You can use this book in a number of different ways:
- Some trainers may ask you to read it before undertaking the qualification.
- It is a good idea to have the book with you in the training session. You can refer to it as needed, and it's a good place to note the answers to any questions you may have, so they're at hand for future reference.
- It is also recommended that you re-read the guide after taking your qualification with a view to seeing what changes you need to make at your premises. You may find the checklists in the 'More Information' section helpful in assessing what steps you should take.

The Scottish Government has introduced training requirements for personal licence holders under the Licensing (Scotland) Act 2005 as part of its response to tackling a huge rise in alcohol problems in Scotland.

So in learning about your key responsibilities and in taking steps to ensure that you and the staff in your premises uphold the law, and in doing what you can to promote responsible drinking, you will be playing a very important part in helping to change Scotland's drinking culture for the better.

Alcohol Focus Scotland has a long history of providing high quality training to the licensed trade through its ServeWise programme. City & Guilds is the UK's leading vocational awarding body, issuing certificates for over two million candidates annually. It has a particular interest in hospitality qualifications.

The two have joined forces, bringing together their complementary strengths, to provide the best platform possible for the provision of the new qualifications.

We hope that you will find this guide interesting and useful.

Licensing law

Licensing law

Know your rights

One of the licence holder's biggest responsibilities is to ensure that alcohol is being sold responsibly and within the law. That means knowing who you can legally sell alcohol to, under what circumstances you can sell it, and who you must refuse to sell to.

It makes good business sense to have lots of satisfied customers, but in certain circumstances refusal is essential. If you do refuse to serve someone, always make sure you are as tactful and polite as possible so that the upset for the refused customer, and those nearby, is minimised. Hopefully, they will see that you are giving responsible and good customer service, and will return another day. Legally, as a licence holder, you are at liberty to refuse to serve anyone, although you should remember that if you refuse anyone on grounds of race, sex or disability, you could land yourself in trouble under discrimination laws. This part of the book sums up the key things you need to know about your responsibilities – and your rights – under the Licensing (Scotland) Act 2005.

Licensing (Scotland) Act 2005

The purpose of liquor licensing is to regulate the sale of alcohol in order to minimise harm.
Scotland has a relatively new Licensing Act - it only came into force in September 2009. When the old law was being reviewed, the Nicholson Committee set up to do this was given the following terms of reference:
· to review all aspects of liquor licensing law and practice in Scotland, with particular reference to the implications for health and public order
· to recommend changes in the public interest, and to report accordingly.

The Licensing (Scotland) Act 2005 came from the recommendations of the Nicholson Committee. The Act sets out five high-level 'licensing objectives'. All have equal weighting and every decision about licensing must be made with reference to these five objectives:

1 preventing crime and disorder
2 securing public safety
3 preventing public nuisance
4 protecting and improving public health
5 protecting children from harm.

Further amendments to licensing legislation were made by the Criminal Justice and Licensing (Scotland) Act 2010 and the Alcohol Etc (Scotland) Act 2010. These changes have been included in this Guidebook.

In the Act 'alcohol' means spirits, wines, beer, cider or any other fermented, distilled or spirituous liquor. It doesn't cover alcohol 0.5% or less, the aromatic flavouring essence angostura bitters or alcohol contained in liqueur confectionery. (For more details, and a full list of what isn't covered, see Part 3 'Alcohol – and its influences'.)

The Act regulates the sale of alcohol. It covers all liquor licensing matters including the licensing objectives, licensing bodies and officers; licensing of premises and people to sell alcohol; licensed hours, control of order and offences on licensed premises.

Licensing officials

The Act aims to directly involve communities in licensing decisions. All of the following play a role in the licensing system.

The Licensing Board

There is one Licensing Board for each council area, or division of a council area. The local council elects members to the Board from among its council members, or councillors. The Board must have between five and ten members – each council decides the number it needs. A Clerk who is a solicitor or advocate is appointed to the Board and is responsible for providing legal advice. Board members must gain a training qualification (roughly one day's training plus an exam).

Licensing Boards have powers under the Licensing Act to determine whether or not to grant new licence applications. This includes premises licences and variations, personal licences and renewals, and occasional licences. They also have the power to determine whether or not there is overprovision of licensed premises, or a particular type of licensed premises, in any locality.

The Licensing Board hears any review of an existing premises or personal licence and decides what action should be taken. In carrying out their functions, Licensing Boards must seek to uphold the five licensing objectives.

The Licensing Board must hold public meetings, which need to be publicised well in advance. The Board is allowed to delegate certain decisions to a

Committee made up of members or to the Clerk, including the granting of occasional licences and personal licences or renewals where there are no offences, and minor variations of a premises licence.

In addition, each Licensing Board must write a statement of its policy, to be published every three years, although the Board can add supplementary statements. They must consult with the Local Licensing Forum, the Health Board and others. The policy:
· must seek to promote the licensing objectives
· can give a general approach to the making of licensing decisions
· should give guidance on the hours that are likely to be granted to types of premises.

Each Licensing Board must also keep a publicly available register, the 'licensing register', which shows full information about all licences and any decisions the Board has made regarding them.

The Local Licensing Forum

Each local council must establish a Local Licensing Forum for their area or division. The functions of the Local Licensing Forum are to:
· review the operation of the Licensing (Scotland) Act 2005 and how the Licensing Board operates in that area
· review the operation of the local Licensing Board's functions.

The Forum also gives advice and makes recommendations to the Board. However, the Forum cannot make recommendations on any particular case. The Licensing Board must have regard to the advice of the Forum and they must give reasons if they choose not to follow it. The Board must also provide statistical information to the Forum if requested.

Forums must meet at least four times per year. Licensing Boards must hold a joint meeting with the Forum at least once per calendar year.

The local council must appoint between five and twenty members to the Forum. These must include people who represent the interests of:

· licence holders
· the chief constable
· persons having health, education or social work functions
· residents of the area
· young people.

The Forum must elect a convener annually. At least one Licensing Standards Officer (LSO) for the council and one person from the relevant Health Board must be a member of the Forum.

Licensing Standards Officers

Each council must appoint one or more Licensing Standards Officers (LSO) for their area, who will report to the Licensing Board, liaise with other council departments and will be a member of the Local Licensing Forum. The LSO must undertake a prescribed training qualification (around three days training plus an exam). The LSO has three main functions.

1 Guidance	Providing information and guidance to interested persons concerning the operation of the Licensing Act in their area, although they cannot give legal advice.
2 Compliance	Monitoring compliance by licence holders.
3 Mediation	Providing mediation services to avoid or resolve disputes or disagreements between licence holders and any other persons.

You must allow an LSO to enter your premises at any time, although they're likely to keep visits to normal opening hours. They can inspect or seize any substances, articles or documents relating to licensing legislation found there. Licence holders, premises managers or anyone working on the premises must provide the LSO with assistance and information, and produce documents as requested. Failure to do so (without reasonable excuse) is an offence.

If an LSO believes a condition of a licence has been breached or has received a complaint from a member of the public, they can investigate the matter and inform you. If not enough is done to resolve the situation, then the LSO will issue a compliance notice requiring the situation be rectified. You must deal with any such notice in the specified timescale. If the matter is not resolved satisfactorily, the LSO can make an application to the Licensing Board for a review of the premises licence (see page 19).

Premises licence

A premises licence is issued by the local Licensing Board in whose area the premises are situated, and authorises the sale of alcohol on the premises. It governs what activities are allowed and what hours the premises can be open for business.

The applicant

To apply for a premises licence, you must be at least 18 years old.

There is a check to see whether applicants for premises licences (and also personal licences, see page 20) have any convictions of a relevant offence or foreign offence (spent convictions are not counted). If you are convicted of a relevant or foreign offence while the application is being processed, you must inform the Licensing Board within one month. If you are charged with an offence, you must inform the court that you are a licence holder, and if convicted then both you as the licence holder and the court have a duty to inform the Licensing Board. It is an offence if you fail to inform either the Licensing Board or the court. In addition, police have the ability to comment to the Licensing Board on an applicant's suitability with regard to the five licensing objectives.

The list of relevant or foreign offences is a long one. Some of those included are violence or sexual offences and statutory offences, including under the Trades Descriptions Act, Food Safety Act, Betting, Gaming and Lotteries Act, Drugs Act, Firearms Act and Traffic Act, as well as common law offences including breach of the peace, contempt of court and perjury. For more information, ask your local Licensing Board.

Did you know?

A premises licence is for the premises where alcohol will be sold. There is no limit on the number of premises licences a company or partnership may hold.

Application process

To ensure you can do everything you want, your application will have to cover all the activities on the premises, whether or not they relate to alcohol. Remember to include all the activities that happen throughout the year.

Your application to the Licensing Board must contain:
- a description of the premises
- a layout plan
- an operating plan
- certificates for planning, building standards and food hygiene if food is supplied
- a disabled access and facilities statement.

Layout plan
Your layout plan must include:
- where alcohol will be sold
- where activities will take place
- any area to which children and young people will have access.

Operating plan
Your operating plan is a detailed plan of how you intend to run your business. In the plan you must include:
- a description of all activities to be carried out
- whether alcohol is to be sold on or off the premises (or both)
- the proposed capacity of the premises
- name and address of the premises manager, who must be a personal licence holder and should be the person taking day-to-day responsibility for the premises (a person cannot be a premises manager for more than one premises at a time)
- (on-licence) whether children will be permitted and, if so, what ages will be permitted, and details of when and where they will be allowed to enter
- core times when alcohol will be sold and any seasonal variations.

If you forget to put anything in your operating plan, you will not be allowed to do it unless you apply for a variation of your licence. On receipt of the application, the Licensing Board will notify neighbours, any community councils, the local council, police and fire authorities. The Board will have a meeting to consider the application, taking into account any objections or representations received from interested parties. Anybody can object to an application, so make friends with your neighbours if you can! Objectors can argue against the licence on any of the five grounds for refusal listed below. The Licensing Board can reject any objection if it is considered frivolous or vexatious.

Did you know?
Representations can be letters in support of the application, or they can ask for changes to the operation plan that the person believes are required or they can ask for conditions that the person believes should be imposed.

Application process for a premises licence

```
                    Apply to the
                    Licensing Board (LB)
                          │
                          ▼
                    LB notifies the police
                    and neighbours

  Any objections made                      Police report to LB on
  to LB and the applicant                  anti-social behaviour
  notified                                 in the area if relevant
                                           or if requested by LB

  LB grants the premises    LB considers the
  licence with conditions   application and any
                            objections to it

  Modifications made        LB asks for          LB refuses the        Accept LB's decision.
  and LB grants the         modifications to     premises licence      Can re-apply after
  licence with conditions   the operating plan   application           one year
                            and/or layout plan

                            Accept LB's decision  Appeal to the Sheriff  Sheriff Principal sends
                            but ask for direction Principal              the case back to LB for
                            to re-apply within                           reconsideration
                            one year

                                                 Sheriff Principal      Sheriff Principal
                                                 reverses LB's          makes another
                                                 decision               decision considered
                                                                        appropriate
```

Grounds for refusal

Licensing Boards can refuse an application on the following grounds:
- the premises in question is an excluded premises (eg a motorway service station)
- the premises are unsuitable for the sale of alcohol
- granting the licence is inconsistent with any of the five licensing objectives
- granting the application would result in overprovision in the locality of the licensed premises
- the same application was refused within the last year and no direction granted.

If no grounds for refusal apply, then the Licensing Board must grant the application. The Licensing Board issues the premises licence and a summary of the licence. Once granted, the premises licence lasts indefinitely, unless revoked, suspended or varied. It's your job to make sure it isn't.

If the application is refused, another application cannot be made within one year for the same premises unless:
- at the time the application was refused a direction was granted by the Licensing Board to allow a resubmission within a year, or
- it can be shown there has been a material change in circumstance.

Beyond this an appeal against a Licensing Board's decision can be made to the Sheriff Principal at the Sheriff's Court, but it is advisable to get legal advice before proceeding as the appeal must be on very specific grounds.

Conditions

Every premises licence has conditions attached. There are three 'levels' of conditions – mandatory national conditions that apply to all premises, national discretionary conditions - also known as pool conditions - and local conditions. The Act gives Scottish Ministers the power to add to the list of national conditions as they feel necessary. Such changes would normally be covered in the licensed trade press and the LSO would also provide advice. The national conditions, plus any local or discretionary conditions applied, become part of the premises licence. Breach of any of the conditions may lead to a review of the licence.

Mandatory conditions for all premises

Mandatory national conditions for both on- and off-licence premises include:

- Alcohol cannot be sold on the premises when there is no named premises manager, or when the premises manager does not hold a personal licence, or when his/her personal licence is suspended, or when his/her licensing qualification does not meet the requirements of the law.
- The premises should be run in accordance with the operating plan.
- Every sale of alcohol must be authorised by the premises manager or another personal licence holder. (They can give a general authorisation for all staff to be able to sell alcohol – they don't have to supervise each sale.)
- All staff (paid or unpaid) who sell alcohol must have been trained and whenever they are working a record of their training must be available on the premises to produce to a Licensing Standards Officer.
- The price of alcohol can only change at the start of the licensed period and the price must stay the same for at least 72 hours. Note: off-sales premises can start individual price changes on different days.
- No irresponsible drinks promotions are allowed (see page 16).
- Premises licence fees must be paid annually to the council.

Mandatory conditions (on-licence)

Mandatory national conditions that apply to on-licence premises only include:

- Staff who serve alcohol (eg waiters and waitresses) must be trained.
- Tap water fit for drinking must be provided free of charge on request.
- All non-alcoholic drinks must be available for purchase at a reasonable price.
- There must be a notice (at least A4 size) displayed so that it is reasonably visible to customers entering the premises, stating whether or not children are permitted on the premises, and if so, where on the premises they are permitted and any conditions relating to them while there.
- For premises that permit admission of children under five, there must be baby-changing facilities that are accessible to persons of either gender (vehicles, vessels and moveable structures are exempted).

Mandatory conditions (off-licence)

Mandatory national conditions applying only to off-licence premises include:

- alcohol can be displayed in only one or both of the following - a single area as agreed between the Licensing Board and the premises licence holder and/or a single area that is not accessible by the public, eg behind the counter.
- multiple purchases must cost at least the same as buying the items individually
- in off-sales premises drinks promotions can only take place in the designated area for alcohol sales or a designated tasting room.

Mandatory conditions for late opening premises

These conditions apply to premises open after 01.00. Between 01.00 and 05.00 (or close, whichever is earlier) they must have a first aider on the prmisese. In addition, premises that have a capacity of 250 or more and provide music, dancing or entertainment must have:
- a personal licence holder on the premises
- written policies on drugs and evacuation of the premises
- CCTV
- monitoring of toilets
- an SIA-qualified door steward at every entrance.

Discretionary conditions

Discretionary conditions are nationally set conditions from which Licensing Boards can choose the one(s) they think relevant to their area or particular premises in their area. At the time of writing, there are none in the list.

Local conditions

Local conditions give Licensing Boards the flexibility to deal with local issues or circumstances. Where they are imposed they must be consistent with mandatory national conditions. Examples of these may be:
- no entry onto the premises after 23.00
- no drinks on the dance floor.

Irresponsible drinks promotions

This list may be added to over time by the Scottish Government. It includes:
- any promotion likely to appeal to a person under 18
- anything that involves a free or reduced price alcoholic drink with the purchase of one (or more) drinks, which don't have to be alcoholic
- anything that involves a free or reduced price measure of an alcoholic drink with the purchase of one (or more) measures of the drink (on-licence only)
- providing unlimited amounts of alcohol for a set price (including the entrance fee) (on-licence only)
- anything that encourages a person to buy or consume larger measures than they had intended (on-licence only)
- anything based on the strength of alcohol
- anything that rewards or encourages people to drink alcohol quickly
- anything that offers alcohol as a prize/reward (unless that alcohol is in a sealed container and then consumed off the premises)

What do you do with your premises licence?

The premises licence holder is responsible for keeping the premises licence, or a certified copy, on the premises and ensuring a summary, or a certified copy, is publicly displayed. The premises licence is an important document with key information including:

- the name and address of the premises manager
- the name and address of the premises licence holder
- a description of the premises for which the licence is issued
- the date on which the licence takes effect
- the operating plan and the layout plan for the premises, including licensed opening hours
- the conditions to which the licence is subject (or a reference to where the conditions can be found).

Don't forget to notify the Licensing Board of any change of name or address of the licence holder or premises manager within one month. Failure to do so is an offence.

Did you know?

Every premises must have a named premises manager. A person can only be the premises manager for one premises at a time and the premises manager must be a personal licence holder. They are responsible for the day-to-day running of the premises.

Transferring a licence to a new owner

When selling licensed premises, the premises licence holder must make an application to the Licensing Board to transfer the premises licence to the new owner, or transferee. A copy is then sent to the chief constable. The chief constable has 21 days to report to the Licensing Board on the transferee.

If the transferee or connected persons have no relevant convictions, the Licensing Board must grant the application. If, however, the chief constable's report shows convictions, a hearing will be arranged to consider the application.

Did you know?

You must inform the Licensing Board of any incoming or outgoing person(s) who are connected to, or are interested parties in, the business within 1 month. You must also notify the Licensing Board of changes in names or addresses - the Board must inform the police.

Variations of a premises licence

Applications for a variation of the premises licence are made to the Licensing Board and must be accompanied by the premises licence. Minor variations have to be granted by the Board. These include:

- variation of the layout plan, as long as the change is still consistent with the operating plan
- restricting the amount of access for under-18s
- any changes relating to the premises manager.

If the premises manager ceases to work for a company, becomes incapable or dies, or has their personal licence revoked or suspended, the premises licence holder must notify the Licensing Board within seven days. They must also make an application within six weeks to vary the licence to substitute a new manager. The applicant should mark on the application that it is to have immediate effect. This will allow the application to be deemed granted and allow the new manager to take up his position straight away. Remember: if there is no active premises manager, no alcohol can be sold.

For all other variations, eg to change a condition of the operating plan such as the opening hours, the Licensing Board must hold a hearing to make a decision. This is very similar to a new licence application and subject to the same grounds for refusal and the same rules for appeal and re-applying.

Alterations

If you are considering any alterations make sure that you have all the required permissions. These include building warrants and planning consent and also you must have obtained a variation of your premises licence.

Review and possible suspension

Anybody may apply to the Licensing Board to have a premises licence reviewed, although they must state why they are applying for the review. It's a good idea to remember this when dealing with disputes with neighbours. The grounds for review are:
- one or more of the conditions have been breached
- the operation of the premises is compromising one or more of the licensing objectives.

The Licensing Board can also initiate this procedure – and so can the LSOs.

Upon receipt of an application the Licensing Board will consider whether the application contains grounds for review and arrange a hearing if necessary. The Board can reject any application to review a premises licence if it is thought to be frivolous or vexatious. If the Board finds, during the review, that you are not complying with certain conditions of your licence or are running the premises in a way that is inconsistent with the licensing objectives, they can take the following steps:
- issue a warning
- make a variation to the licence (such as reducing your opening hours)
- suspend or revoke the licence.

Any concerned members of the public apply to LB for review of the premises licence

LB has concerns and initiates a review of the premises licence

LSO has concerns and talks with the premises licence holder

Nothing or not enough done

Matter resolved

LSO issues compliance notice

Nothing or not enough done

Matter resolved

LSO applies for review of the licence

LB holds a hearing to review the premises licence

Problems identified with personal licence holder and his/her licence reviewed

Nothing found

Problems identified

Revoke the premises licence

Suspend the premises licence

Issue a written warning to the premises licence holders

Vary the premises licence

Did you know?

Any person can be a personal licence holder if they meet the requirements.

Personal licence

As a personal licence holder you can authorise the sale of alcohol. Every premises must have one premises manager and the premises manager must be a personal licence holder. Most premises, however, are likely to employ several personal licence holders to ensure there is always a qualified person present.

Training required

The 2005 Act requires that a personal licence holder must have a suitable qualification. The Scottish Government has specified the content of personal licence holder training. It must be a nominal ten hours of training – generally a one-day course, plus some home study, followed by a multiple-choice exam. It must cover:
- an introduction to licensing
- responsible operation of licensed premises
- the effect of irresponsible operation on society and health.

Personal licence holder trainers must be trained to a national agreed standard of competency: they have to have a training qualification and demonstrate an awareness of licensing law in Scotland attained in the last three years.

Application process

An application for a personal licence should be made to the Licensing Board for the area that the applicant normally lives in (even if the person works in premises covered by a different Board). The Licensing Board will notify the chief constable. The application must include two photos of the applicant and the appropriate fee. The Licensing Board must grant the application as long as:
- the applicant is 18 or over and has a suitable licensing qualification
- the applicant has not had a licence revoked in the last five years
- the applicant is not already in posession of a (Scottish) Personal Licence
- the chief constable has not issued a notice advising that the applicant has relevant convictions or indicated that the applicant is not suitable with regards to the five licensing objectives. The same obligations to inform the Board of any relevant or foreign offences apply as for the application for a premises licence (see page 11). If the applicant has convictions the Board must hold a hearing to determine the application.

There is no mechanism for anyone other than the police to object to a personal licence application. Once granted, the licence will last for ten years, unless suspended or revoked. You must update your qualification every five years and advise the Licensing Board accordingly.

Application process for a personal licence

Apply to the Licensing Board (LB)

↓

LB notifies the police

Police reply to LB that applicant has no convictions

Police report that applicant has convictions or object under 1 of the 5 objectives

LB considers the application and finds all requirements met

LB considers the application

LB grants personal licence

LB is satisfied and grants personal licence

LB is not satisfied and application is refused

What do you do with your licence?

The personal licence will show name and address of the licence holder, the Licensing Board, expiry date and any relevant or foreign offence. As a personal licence holder, you must be able to produce your licence to either the police or the LSO when working on licensed premises. You also have a duty to notify the Licensing Board of any changes to your name or address within one month. Failure to do so would be an offence. It is also an offence if you fail to notify the Licensing Board of a relevant or foreign conviction.

A licence is counted as void if it has been lost or stolen, or revoked and all void licences must be returned to the Licensing Board. It is an offence to try to pass off a void licence as a valid one.

The police can report a personal licence holder to the Licencing Board for conduct inconsistent with the licensing objectives. The Licensing Board must then hold a hearing.

Did you know?

An endorsement on a personal licence works a bit like points on a driving licence. An endorsement lasts five years and if a personal licence holder gains three endorsements, the Licensing Board must hold a hearing to review the licence.

Renewal of a personal licence

Personal licence holders must apply for a renewal at least three months before the expiry date to the Licensing Board that originally issued the licence. The application should include the personal licence or, if not practical, a statement of the reasons why it could not be sent.

If problems are found with the personal licence holder, the licence can be reviewed (see page 23). The problems might be identified as part of the review of a premises licence. If nothing is found, the personal licence holder keeps the licence. If problems are identified, the licence can be revoked, endorsed or suspended.

Other types of licence

Occasional licence

This allows alcohol to be sold on an unlicensed premises on particular dates. Applications can be made by either a personal or premises licence holder or a representative from any voluntary organisation. Members' clubs and voluntary organisations are restricted to no more than four licences lasting four days or more, and twelve licences lasting less than four days, up to a maximum of fifty-six days in any twelve-month period.

The Licensing Board can impose limits on occasional licenses issued to an individual or premises.

Temporary licence

The issue of a temporary licence allows a business to continue to operate in another premises while its normal premises are undergoing reconstruction or conversion.

Review of a personal licence

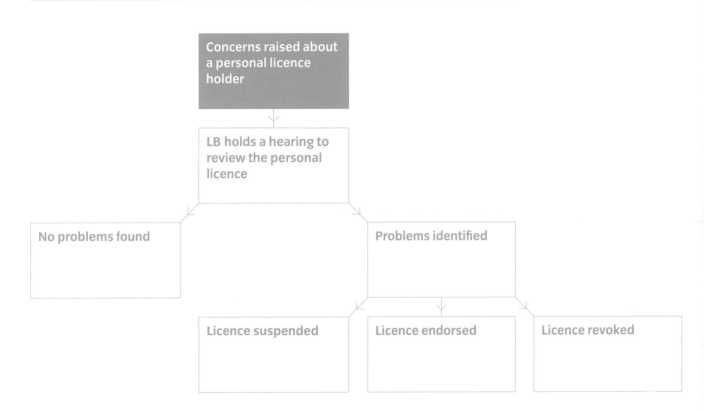

Provisional licence

A provisional licence can be granted to premises that will be, or are being, built or converted. It is valid for 4 years.

Members' clubs

Members' clubs are included in the same system of licensing and subject to the same rules as other licensed premises, with a couple of exceptions:
- They are required to have a premises licence, although they do not have to name a premises manager. This means that they will not require a personal licence holder to authorise the sale of alcohol.
- The Licensing Board will not include them in any assessment of overprovision.

Members' clubs are able to apply for occasional licences (see page 22). On these occasions the premises can be opened to members of the public.

Licensed hours

Off-licence premises

Alcohol can be sold in off-licence premises from 10.00 to 22.00, Monday to Sunday. The Licensing Board must refuse any application that asks for off-sales outside these times. It is possible that a Licensing Board may restrict off-sales hours for particular premises if there are problems, or to fit with local circumstances.

On-licence premises

On-licences will have licensed hours (ie the times when they can sell alcohol) determined by the hours stated in the operating plan and hours will be specific to each premises. Some Licensing Boards insist that premises are open for the hours stated in the operating plan and granted in the premises licence, but many do not. Check with your Board or LSO. The Licensing Board must refuse any request for 24-hour opening unless there are exceptional circumstances.

Extended hours (on-licence)

A premises licence holder can apply to the Licensing Board for an extension of licensed hours for their premises for a special event or occasion. The Licensing Board must notify the police and the LSO for the area when any application is made and if it is granted. In addition, Licensing Boards may grant general extensions of licensing hours for an event of local or national significance, for all or some of the on-licence premises in the area as the Board decides. The Licensing Board can vary the conditions of the premises licence for the period of the extended hours.

Exceptions to licensed hours

There are exceptions to the hours permitted in your operating plan. The main ones are listed below. All of these are optional; you do not have to allow them.

Drinking-up time	A period of fifteen minutes is allowed at the end of hours for consuming any remaining alcohol that has been bought during licensed hours.
Meals	If alcohol was supplied with a meal, then the drinking-up time increases to thirty minutes.
Residents	Hotel residents or their guests can drink alcohol and take it away at any time but the alcohol can only be sold to the resident.

British Summer Time

Premises open at the time that the clocks go forward/back should ignore the change to the clock and trade for the usual amount of hours.

Staff training

The Licensing (Scotland) Act 2005 requires that all staff who serve or sell alcohol are trained. This includes full-time, part-time and casual staff and people who are unpaid. The training must cover an agreed syllabus – set by the Scottish Government – that includes the basics of licensing law, alcohol and the influence of environment in licensed premises. This training can be delivered in a number of ways.

- A personal licence holder or trained trainer can deliver suitable training.
- Staff could use a workbook under the supervision of a personal licence holder. City & Guilds and ServeWise have produced the Workbook for Staff of Licensed Premises for this purpose. (For details on ordering, see the 'More information' section at the back of this book.)

•Staff could undertake formal training to gain a nationally recognised training certificate such as the 'Certificate for Staff Working in Scottish Licensed Premises', available from ServeWise and City & Guilds, which normally includes about four hours of training and an exam. (To find out more, see the list of courses in the 'More information' section.)

A training log must be kept with the names and signatures of both the person undertaking the training and the trainer. The trainer must also note their qualification. They may be either a personal licence holder, in which case they should give the name of the Licensing Board that granted the licence, or they may hold a relevant training qualification. The qualification should be accredited by the Scottish Qualifications Authority. They should give the name of the qualification they hold and the company they're employed by. One of the roles of the LSO is to check that premises are complying with the law, and it is probable that a visiting LSO will need to see these training records.

Protecting children from harm

Did you know?

The Licensing (Scotland) Act 2005 defines a child as being under 16 years of age, a young person as being 16 or 17, and an adult as being 18 or over.

One of your biggest responsibilities as a licence holder is to ensure that alcohol is being sold responsibly and within the law. It is a key responsibility that you do not sell alcohol to anyone under the age of 18. With trendy clothes and the stylish makeup some girls wear, it's often very difficult to tell what age your potential customer is. So what can you do to protect yourself from prosecution?

No proof of age, no sale

The 2005 Act states that the server must be able to show that they believed the person to be 18 or over and that either:
•no reasonable person would suspect from the person's appearance that he or she was under 18, or
•they asked the person for proof of age (and what they were shown appeared to be an appropriate form of proof of age and one that would have convinced a reasonable person).

The Act says that acceptable forms of proof of age are a passport, a European photocard driving licence, a photographic identity card approved by the Proof of Age Standards Scheme (PASS) or any other document as may be prescribed. Check with the Licensing Officer at your local police office or the LSO. The most commonly available proof of age card in Scotland is the Young Scot card. Always check for the holographic PASS logo and, as with all forms of proof of age, check the date of birth.

Display notice

Under the 2005 Act, premises must display a notice regarding underage sales. It must be displayed at all times and be visible to any person seeking to purchase alcohol. The notice must be A4 size or larger and must contain:

> It is an offence for any person under the age of 18 to buy or attempt to buy alcohol on these premises.
>
> It is also an offence for any other person to buy or attempt to buy alcohol on these premises for a person under the age of 18.
>
> Where there is doubt as to whether a person attempting to buy alcohol on these premises is age 18 or over, alcohol will not be sold to the person except on production of evidence showing the person to be 18 or over.

Prevention system and refusals book

The law now states that you must have an age verification policy in place where everyone who appears to be under 25 is asked for proof of age. It is also good practice to have:

- signage for staff and customers about what forms of proof of age are accepted
- proof that you and your staff refuse sales, eg by recording all refusals in a refusals book.

You should check that all of your staff know how to use the refusals book. If one person is not using it properly, then they might need training on who to refuse service to and how to do it. Keep your refusals book at the counter/bar and make sure everyone fills it in when refusing a sale. If you get a visit from the police, you can easily produce it to show how you comply with the law. The refusals book could also contain some brief reminder points on who cannot be served alcohol and brief tips on handling the situation when you refuse a customer. It is possible to buy specially designed refusal books, such as the ServeWise Refusals Book, which includes all of these things. (See the 'More information' section at the back for further details.)

Offences relating to under-18s

It is an offence for licence holders and staff to:
- sell alcohol to a person under 18, or for a responsible person to allow it

- sell liqueur confectionery to a person under 16
- allow a person under 18 to sell, supply or serve alcohol unless:
  - in an off-licence premises, the sale is specifically approved by a person 18 or over
  - in an on-licence premises, the alcohol is for consumption with a meal and the supply or service is specifically approved by a person 18 or over
- allow a person under 18 to consume alcohol on licensed premises (but see exception below)
- deliver alcohol to a person under 18 (unless part of their job is to take in deliveries) or for a responsible person to allow it to be delivered
- allow a person under 18 to deliver alcohol (unless it's part of their job) or for a responsible person to allow it to be delivered.

It is an offence for customers to:
- buy, or attempt to buy, alcohol if they are under the age of 18 (unless it's part of a test purchasing scheme)
- buy alcohol for a child/young person under 18 (but see exception below)
- allow a person under 18 to consume alcohol on licensed premises
- send a person under 18 to obtain alcohol.

Exceptions (on-licence)

Although you cannot legally sell alcohol to a person who is 16 or 17 years old under any circumstances, you can allow them to consume alcohol bought by an adult if it is to accompany a meal. Only beer, cider, wine or perry is allowed and only in limited amounts. You have no obligation to serve them, but legally, you are permitted to do so. It's always a good idea to have a house policy that sets out your rules on this and other matters. Make sure that your staff are aware of your house policy. For guidance on developing a house policy, see the 'More information' section .

Test purchasing

Test purchasing allows the police to send someone under 18 years old into licensed premises to try to buy alcohol to check that the premises does not sell alcohol to underagers. There is a strict code of conduct governing a test purchasing scheme. This aims to protect the welfare of the child or young person, and also aims to make the system fair for the licence holder and staff. The underage person is not allowed to try to look older than their real age and must tell the truth if they are asked what age they are.

Other offences

We've already seen some of the offences relating to children and young people. There are other offences that you also need to be aware of. It is an offence for licence holders, staff or any 'responsible person' to:
- sell alcohol to a person who is drunk
- be drunk on the premises
- allow a breach of the peace, drunkenness or other disorderly conduct on the premises
- keep smuggled goods on licensed premises
- deliver alcohol to a private address between the hours of midnight and 06.00
- fail to display the notice regarding underage sales
- fail to display a summary of the licence.

It is an offence for customers:
- to attempt to enter any licensed premises while drunk (unless the person resides there)
- to be on licensed premises while drunk and incapable of looking after themselves
- to obtain or attempt to obtain alcohol for a drunk person or to help a drunk person obtain alcohol
- for a drunk person to behave in a disorderly manner
- for a drunk person to use obscene or indecent language to the annoyance of any other person
- for a person to behave in a disorderly manner and refuse to leave when asked to do so by a responsible person. (A responsible person can use reasonable force if necessary to remove the person from the premises.)

So what is drunk exactly?

There is no legal definition, so it is up to you to decide. But do remember that you may put your personal licence and possibly even the premises licence at stake if you serve a drunken person. Therefore, if in doubt, don't serve them. (We will look at signs of drunkenness in Part 3 and ways of refusing service in Part 4.)

As we are all subject to the law of the land, don't assume that because something isn't listed in this book, it doesn't apply to you. A criminal conviction can affect your fitness to hold a personal or premises licence.

Did you know?

A responsible person is defined as the premises manager or occasional licence holder or any person aged 18 or over who has the authority to sell alcohol or the authority to stop any offence from occurring.

Additional areas

Deliveries

If you sell alcohol for delivery to a customer you must ensure that the sale takes place within licensed hours. No deliveries must take place between midnight and 06.00. You must also keep a day book (kept at the premises) and a delivery book or invoice (kept with the delivery) that states the quantity, description and price of the alcohol and the name and address of the person it is being delivered to. Remember that it's an offence for alcohol to be delivered to a child or young person. It is also an offence for alcohol to be delivered by a child or young person unless he or she works on the premises in a capacity which involves the delivery of alcohol.

Rights of entry

Police can enter and inspect licensed premises (including off-sales and members' clubs) at any time and obstructing a police officer from doing so constitutes an offence. LSOs can also enter and inspect premises at any time. Obstructing or refusing to comply without reasonable excuse is an offence.

Exclusion orders

An exclusion order is an order made by the court excluding a particular person from a particular licensed premises (or group of licensed premises) and lasts between three months and two years. It applies to a person convicted of a violent offence committed on or in the vicinity of licensed premises. If an order is not imposed by the court at the time, the premises licence holder has up to six weeks after the date of conviction to apply to have the order imposed. Anyone entering licensed premises in breach of an exclusion order commits an offence and is liable to receive a fine, a term of imprisonment or both.

Closure orders and emergency closure orders

Licensing Boards can make a closure order requiring the premises to close at the request of a police officer (of the rank of inspector or above) if there is a likelihood of disorder on or in the vicinity of the premises and the order is in the interest of public safety.

Police officers (of the rank of inspector or above) also have the power to make emergency closure orders that can last for up to 24 hours. These can be extended for a further 24 hours if required. There are two ways in which a closure order can be terminated.

- A police officer (of the rank of inspector or above) must terminate the closure order if satisfied that it's no longer in the interest of public safety. Notice of the termination must be given to a responsible person, and if the closure order was made by the Licensing Board, then the Board must be given notice.
- A Licensing Board may lift the closure order on application of the premises licence holder or occasional holder or if it is satisfied that it is no longer in the interest of public safety.

Vessels, vehicles and moveable structures

It is an offence to sell alcohol on a moving vehicle unless it has a premises or an occasional licence. An example would be a party limousine. Ferries or trains that are engaged on a journey do not need a licence to sell alcohol. However, if a ferry was permanently moored, it would need to be licensed.

Safeguarding your licence

Do people get charged under the licensing laws? In a word, yes. Even where an offence does not lead to a criminal prosecution, it may still be brought to the attention of the Licensing Board who can review the personal and premises licences.

Under a system of vicarious liability, the premises licence holder or interested party can be charged for an offence than an employee or agent commits, even if the employee or agent is not charged. Licence holders therefore need to show that they actively take steps to prevent offences from occurring. These could be set out in a house or store policy and covered in staff induction training.

Your house policy can give staff guidance on how you do things in your premises. But it's not enough to train staff on arrival and give them a copy of house policy. Your staff need to understand and abide by the policies in place, and take part in continuous training. You should also test your system – how else can you know that your staff are doing what you asked? It's your licence that will be revoked or suspended, so there's a lot riding on it. Don't be careless about it.

Self check

1 What are the five licensing objectives of the Licensing (Scotland) Act 2005?

2 Name the two main types of licence available under the new law.

3 What document demonstrates how you plan to run your business?

4 Who can object to a premises licence application?

5 What are the licensed hours for the following:

a Off-licence premises?

b On-licence premises?

6 Who can authorise the sale of alcohol?

7 What types of 'proof of age' are acceptable?

8 The police have the right to enter your premises at any time. Which other licensing official has the right of entry?

9 Name three offences that can be committed by:

a staff or licence holders

b customers.

Test practice

1 Which one of the following is the body that grants premises and personal licence applications, renewals and transfers?

a The Environmental Health Office
b The Planning Department
c The Licensing Board
d The Local Licensing Forum

2 Which one of the following people can an occasional licence be granted to?

a A premises licence holder, a personal licence holder or a representative of a voluntary organisation
b Anyone who works in a bar or club selling alcohol
c Members of registered clubs, members of proprietary clubs and representatives of registered charities
d Anyone running an event which is on a not-for-profit basis

3 On which of the following grounds can a member of the public apply for a review of a premises licence?

a The premises is not meeting one of the licensing objectives
b The Licensing Standards Officer has issued a compliance notice
c The staff were rude to them when they visited
d There is overprovision of premises of that type in the area

4 Which one of the following does the applicant for a personal licence have a duty to inform if they are convicted of a relevant or foreign offence while their licence application is being processed?

a The police
b The Licensing Board
c The Local Council
d A Sheriff Principal

5 A personal licence holder must undertake training

a only when applying for the first time for a licence
b yearly
c every five years
d every ten years.

6 Which one of the following indicates where and when a notice relating to the sale of alcohol to underagers in the prescribed form must be displayed?

a At the front of the premises when the premises is open
b At each place where sales of alcohol are made and at all times
c In a non-public area where staff have their break and at all times
d On the till receipt given to customers after a sale of alcohol

7 Which one of the following indicates how it would be found out that a closure order has been terminated and the premises may open again?

a The police must give notice to the LSO
b The police must give notice to a person responsible for the premises
c The LSO must give notice to a person responsible for the premises
d The LSO must give notice to the Licensing Board

2

Other key legislation

The following section will guide you through some of the other laws that affect licensed premises. There are so many laws that not all of them have been included here. Most of the laws and regulations that are listed do require some action by premises managers or personal licence holders, but it is also important that all other members of staff are aware of their legal responsibilities.

Health and safety legislation

Health and Safety at Work Act 1974

The Health and Safety at Work Act 1974 is the principle legislation in this area. It requires employers to ensure, as far as possible, the health, safety and welfare at work of all their employees. It also states that each member of staff is responsible for ensuring that their own working practices will maintain the health and safety of themselves and their colleagues. All staff should have access to written information outlining their responsibilities and those of their employers, which could take the form of either a poster in the staff area or an individual handout.

Management of Health and Safety at Work Regulations 1999

The Management of Health and Safety at Work Regulations 1999 makes more explicit what employers are required to do in order to manage health and safety under the Health and Safety at Work Act 1974. Like the Act, this applies to every work activity.

The duties of the employer are qualified in the Act by the principle of 'so far as is reasonably practicable'. In other words, the degree of risk in a particular job or workplace needs to be balanced against the time, trouble, cost and physical difficulty of taking measures to avoid or reduce the risk.

An employer's main requirement is to carry out a risk assessment, which should be straightforward in licensed premises. A risk assessment identifies potential risks or hazards and how to reduce them. Employers with five or more employees need to record the significant findings of the assessment.

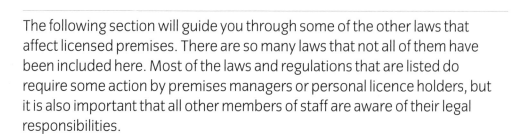

The five steps of risk assessment:
1 look for the hazards (ie anything that could harm the health or endanger the safety of people on the premises)
2 decide who might be harmed and how
3 evaluate the risks and decide whether the existing precautions are adequate or whether more should be done
4 record your findings and implement them
5 review your assessment and revise it, if necessary. Reviews should take place at regular intervals as conditions may change.

The HSE leaflet, *Five Steps to Risk Assessment*, will give you more information. The HSE also publishes guides to good practice and advice on how to comply with the law. See www.hse.gov.uk.

As well as carrying out a risk assessment, employers need to:
- make arrangements for implementing the health and safety measures identified as necessary by the risk assessment
- appoint competent people (often themselves or company colleagues) to implement the arrangements
- set up emergency procedures
- provide clear information and training to employees
- work together with other employers sharing the workplace.

Control of Noise at Work Regulations 2005

Did you know?

Surveys of pub premises show that many have noise levels that regularly exceed 85 dB(A).

Noise levels are measured in decibel units known as dB(A). Damage risk to hearing depends on the noise level and how long people are exposed to it.

You, as an employer, are required to assess your employees' exposure to noise. There is likely to be a problem if:
- people have to shout at each other at normal speaking distance
- anyone goes home with a ringing sensation in their ears.

Where employees are regularly exposed to noise levels of 80 dB(A) or above, employers must assess the risk to workers' health and provide them with information and training. At 85 dB(A), employers must provide hearing protection. Over 85 dB(A), health surveillance (hearing checks) must be provided. See www.hse.gov.uk/noise for more information.

Food, drink and sales legislation

Food Safety Act 1990

These regulations cover every aspect of the safety of food that is intended for human consumption. They apply to off-licences that provide sandwiches, hot snacks or deli counters and, because alcoholic and non-alcoholic drink is classified as a 'food', they apply to all bar staff, regardless of whether they handle meals or not. Servers are recommended to receive some form of elementary food hygiene training. Since the regulations were updated in 1995, anyone who handles food is required to have supervision, instruction and/or practical hygiene training to a level appropriate to their job.

You can commit an offence under the Act if you sell, or keep for eventual sale, food that:
· is unfit for human consumption
· has been rendered injurious to health (or made injurious to health by you)
· is contaminated so that it would be unreasonable to expect it to be eaten
· is not of the nature, substance or quality demanded by the purchaser
· is falsely or misleadingly presented.
(These are only some of the things covered by the Act; this is not a full statement or interpretation of the law.)

The Act contains tough powers to require improvements to be made to unhygienic premises, and premises can be closed where public health is being put at risk. It is mostly enforced by local authority officers, such as Environmental Health Officers, who have the power to enter food premises and inspect food, take samples for investigation and withdraw suspect food.

Full guidance concerning all the requirements can be obtained from the Environmental Health Office at your local council, and it is normally provided free of charge.

Adulteration of food and drink

The Food Safety Act says that it is illegal to add anything harmful to food or drink. It is also illegal to take anything away from it by diluting it or watering it down. Watering down spirits or other alcohol is one example of an offence.

Food hygiene certificates

Under the Licensing Act (Scotland) 2005, you must provide a copy of a Food Hygiene Certificate when applying for your premises licence to the Licensing Board if food will be supplied on the premises. Food Hygiene Certificates will normally be granted by the Environmental Health Office of your local council,

providing that the structural requirements of the food hygiene regulations have been, or will be, met.

The Food Labelling Regulations 1996

These Regulations aim to ensure that foods are correctly labelled. Most foods require an indication of minimum durability such as a 'best before' or a 'use by' date. It is not illegal to sell food after its 'best before' date has passed, but if the product has deteriorated so that it is 'not of the nature, substance or quality demanded by the purchaser' as required under the Food Safety Act, then a prosecution could be brought under the Act. 'Use by' dates are different from 'best before' dates and it is illegal to sell food after its 'use by' date. Some foods do not need to be marked with an indication of durability. These include:

- fresh fruit and vegetables
- wine, liqueur wine, aromatized wine and any similar drink obtained from fruit other than grapes
- any drink with an ABV (alcohol by volume) of 10% or more.

Age-restricted products

Alcohol and liqueur chocolates are among a much longer list of products that can be sold only to customers above a set age.

Over 18 years old	Alcohol, fireworks (includes caps), butane gas/lighter fuel, adult magazines, offensive weapons (knives), cigarettes, tobacco, tobacco-related products
Over 16 years old	Lottery tickets and scratch cards, liqueur chocolates, party poppers, fuel
Depends on classification	Videos, DVDs, games.

Trade Descriptions Act 1968

Under the Trade Descriptions Act, it is an offence to apply a false or misleading description to goods. In other words, the goods you give a customer must be what is advertised. For example, in an on-licence premises, you can't put another brand of gin into a Gordon's gin bottle. Or, in an off-licence, you can't advertise a promotion on 'bottles of spirits', and then say to a customer that

it doesn't include malt whisky. Also, if a customer asks for a particular brand, eg Bell's whisky, and you don't have it, you must check if it is okay with the customer before you give them another brand of whisky.

Protected terms

Certain products are referred to by protected terms that must be used correctly.

Champagne	Only wines grown in the Champagne region of France made by the Champagne method may be legally called Champagne. You must not sell any other sparking wine as 'Champagne'. Similarly, 'Cava' must come from Spain and 'Prosecco' from Italy.
Sherry	This is a legally protected term for fortified wines from Jerez in Spain. Wines from other regions or countries that used to be called sherry now have to be labelled and referred to as 'fortified wine', not sherry. (If they were bottled before 1996, they must be qualified by the country of origin, eg Cyprus Sherry.)
Whisky	The Scotch Whisky Act 1988 makes it an offence to sell as Scotch Whisky any whisky that is not made in Scotland and at least 40% ABV. Similar drinks made in any other country are normally spelt as 'whiskey'.

Non-alcoholic and low alcohol

You must be careful when using the terms non-alcoholic and low alcohol, as each has a specific meaning according to the amount of alcohol present in a drink. For example, you can't give someone a low alcohol drink if they have asked for a non-alcoholic one, unless you check that this is acceptable with them. Please remember, for medical or religious reasons, some people cannot tolerate any alcohol at all. All of the following have specific meanings.

Non-alcoholic	Less than 0.05% alcohol	Beer, cider and wine
De-alcoholised	0.05% – 0.5% alcohol	Beer, cider and wine
Low alcohol	0.5% – 1.2% alcohol	Beer, cider and wine
Reduced alcohol	1.2% – 5% alcohol	Wine

Some shandies can be sold as soft drinks in unlicensed shops. They do not come under licensing law because their alcohol content is under 0.5%. Therefore, they can be bought by children of any age. However, the majority of the general public do not know this. What might they think if they see you selling cans of shandy to children?

Advertising standards

Any form of advertising must conform to an industry set code of practice. If the code of practice is not followed, then it is likely that the government will introduce laws to replace the current system of self-regulation.

There are specific rules for the advertising and promoting of alcohol.

1 Advertisements should be socially responsible and should not encourage excessive drinking.
2 Advertisements should not suggest that any alcoholic drink can enhance mental, physical or sexual capabilities, popularity, attractiveness, masculinity, femininity or sporting achievements.
3 Advertisements must contain nothing that is likely to lead people to adopt styles of drinking that are unwise.
4 Drinking alcohol should not be portrayed as a challenge, nor should it be suggested that people who drink are brave, tough or daring for doing so.
5 Particular care should be taken to ensure that advertisements for sales promotions requiring multiple purchases do not actively encourage excessive consumption.

These rules apply to you, even if you're only putting an advert in the local newspaper or producing a promotional flyer to give out in your local area.

Anyone can make complaints about advertising. Complaints can be made on various grounds. The most common are that the advert:
• would cause serious or widespread offence
• encourages excessive drinking
• is targeted at under-18s
• suggests alcohol could enhance sexual capability.

There are two bodies that govern the advertising and promoting of alcohol, each dealing with different types of advertising. These are:
• Advertising Standards Authority (ASA), which deals with non-broadcasting advertising (press, posters, commercial e-mails, sms) and TV, radio and cinema advertising.
• The Portman Group, which deals with complaints about the naming,

packaging and promotional material (including point of sale materials, websites, sponsorship, press releases, branded merchandise and sampling). Contact details for both are given in the 'More information' section.

Weights and Measures Act 1985 (on-licence only)

All optics and beer measuring devices must comply with specific regulations and be made in compliance with a current certificate of pattern approval. If in doubt, check with the Trading Standards Officer at your local council.

Draught beer and cider	Glasses for draught beer and cider must be government stamped (unless you're using an approved measuring device). Beer and cider may only be sold in quantities of $1/3$ pint, $1/2$ pint and multiples of $1/2$ pint. Following the Metrication Amendment in 1994, only draught beer and cider can be sold in half pints or pints. If you wish to sell shandies or non-alcoholic drinks in a similar quantity, you can use the metric equivalents of 568 ml (approximately one pint) or 284 ml (approximately $1/2$ pint) provided that:
	• you inform the customer • if the drink is advertised in a price list, the metric measure is stated.
Spirits – whisky, gin, vodka and rum	Since 31 December 1994, the only permissible optic measure for the sale of these four spirits is metric. These are available in two sizes: 25 ml and 35 ml, but one size must be chosen for use. It is not legal to use both measures for these spirits on the same premises. A notice stating the size of measure that whisky, vodka, gin and rum are sold in must be clearly displayed.
Cocktails	Any of whisky, vodka, gin or rum are exempt from the above requirements if they form part of a drink which is a mixture of three or more liquids.
Other drinks	Other spirits such as brandy and liqueurs, and fortified wines such as vermouth (eg Martini) and sherry, can be sold in different quantities. If spirits and fortified wines are sold in a measure, it must be metric and government stamped.

At the time of writing, changes were being proposed to allow 2/3 of pints (schooners) and smaller measures of wines and fortified wines. These are expected in 2011.

Wines

Wines can be sold by the glass, bottle or carafe. You can display the information regarding the quantities of wine you offer for sale in every wine list or menu, or on a prominently displayed notice. Since 31 December 1994, wines sold by the glass can only be allowed in measured quantities of 125 ml or 175 ml or multiples of these. Carafes of wine may be sold in quantities of 250 ml, 500 ml, 750 ml and 1 litre.

Consumer Protection Act 1987

This Act prohibits the sale of unsafe goods and makes it an offence to give misleading price indications. All consumer goods, goods used in the workplace and food are covered by the Consumer Protection Act, which sets out the powers available to the enforcement authorities to deal with unsafe products. The primary responsibility for day-to-day enforcement of safety legislation falls under local authority trading standards departments. If you were to fail to meet the requirements made under the Act, it could result in you getting fined up to £5000 and/or a prison term of up to six months. For more information about this act, contact Consumer Direct on 08454 04 05 06 or visit www.consumerdirect.gov.uk.

Business legislation

Disability Discrimination Act 1995

This Act makes it unlawful to discriminate against disabled people in a range of activities. Disability is defined as having 'a physical or mental impairment which has a substantial and long-term adverse effect on a person's ability to carry out normal day-to-day activities'.

Licence holders need to be aware that the Act impacts on employment and the provision of goods, facilities and services. You must make reasonable adjustments to accommodate disabled people.

There are a number of things that you can do:
- make sure that all staff are aware of the Act and provide training in how to meet the needs of disabled customers
- use contrasting colours in doorways, menus, etc, to help visually impaired people
- ensure that pathways outside your premises are kept clear

- mark steps inside or outside your building clearly – such as with a contrasting colour along the edge
- make sure that doors are easy to open and preferably use handles that are easy to grip – this may benefit older customers or those with arthritis
- ensure that entrance mats are flush to avoid a potential tripping hazard
- maximise lighting by ensuring that all windows, lamps and blinds are kept clean
- add extra lighting in potentially hazardous areas, such as stairwells.

Also, common sense and courtesy are always good practice; for example, if you look straight at a customer when you are speaking to them, it will be easier for a person who is hearing impaired to read your lips, or you could offer to guide visually impaired customers to an appropriate seat or area of the premises.

The Equality and Human Rights Commission provides information and advice both to disabled people on their rights and to service providers on their duties under the Act. Various publications giving more detailed guidance are available from the website: www.equalityhumanrights.com.

Smoking, Health and Social Care (Scotland) Act 2005

Under the Smoking, Health and Social Care (Scotland) Act 2005 that came into effect on 26 March 2006, you are not allowed to smoke in enclosed public places in Scotland. These places include pubs, bars, clubs, shops and storerooms. (There is a limited exception for designated hotel bedrooms.) It is an offence to smoke in an enclosed public place (£50 fixed penalty fine) and it is an offence to allow another person to smoke in an enclosed public place (£200 fixed penalty fine). You must display no-smoking signage at every entrance to your premises, in toilets and staff areas.

You are not under any obligation to provide exterior smoking areas or stubbing-out bins for customers or staff. You must, however, think about how failing to provide these will impact on your premises: increased litter, noise, as well as people crowding your entrance, perhaps preventing others from entering. You may want to consider providing designated exterior smoking areas with adequate facilities for the disposal of cigarette butts. You could even put up notices asking your customers to be aware of the noise they make outside so as not to disturb the neighbours.

The Environmental Health Departments of local councils enforce the legislation. For more details, you can check the Scottish Executive's website: www.clearingtheairscotland.com.

Equalities

You cannot discriminate against any member of staff because of their sex/gender, sexual orientation, race, age, marital status, religion, because they have undergone (or intend to undergo) gender reassignment or because of pregnancy or for taking maternity leave. Further, both staff and managers have the right to work in an environment free from intimidation, bullying and harassment – by other staff members or managers, or even customers. Any customer who is behaving in an inappropriate manner should be asked to leave the premises. An employer can be found responsible if a customer or contractor bullies or harasses an employee.

Equal opportunities apply to recruitment, treatment in the job, chances for promotion and training, dismissal or redundancy. You, as an employer, must not label jobs as being 'for men' or 'for women' except in very special circumstances: a person's gender can be considered a 'genuine occupational qualification' in specific jobs, such as acting, or for reasons of decency.

Under the Equality Act 2010, everyone must be paid the same when they are doing the same or similar work. In relation to pay, you must not discriminate against staff on the basis of gender. Staff have the right to discuss their pay with each other. More information can be found on www.equalities.gov.uk.

Security Industry Authority (SIA)

If you work in one of the roles listed below in England, Wales or Scotland or employ someone who works in one of the roles, you may need an SIA licence. From 1 November 2007 in Scotland it became illegal to undertake a licensable activity without an SIA licence. This covers manned guarding, including:
- cash and valuables in transit
- close protection
- door supervision
- public space surveillance CCTV
- security guard
- key holding.

There are two types of licence:
- A front-line licence is required if you are undertaking designated licensable activity (this also covers undertaking non front-line activity). A front-line licence is in the form of a credit card-sized plastic card that must be worn, subject to the licence conditions.
- A non-front-line licence is required if you manage, supervise and/or employ individuals who engage in designated licensable activity, as long as you do not carry out front-line activity yourself. A non front-line licence is issued in the form of a letter.

If your job includes door supervision activities, you need to have a door supervisor licence. It doesn't matter whether you own the licensed premises, are employed by the licensed premises or are employed by a firm which supplies door supervisors to the premises.

A door supervisor licence is required if manned guarding activities are undertaken in relation to on-licensed premises only (when the premises are open to the public, at times when alcohol is being supplied for consumption, or when regulated entertainment is being provided on the premises). A door supervisor licence is not required if the activity:
- only involves the use of CCTV equipment
- falls within the definition of cash and valuables transit
- falls within the definition of close protection (bodyguard).

In Scotland door supervisors are more commonly known as door stewards. For more information on how to get a licence, please visit the SIA website: www.the-sia.org.uk. Also see the list of related qualifications in the 'More information' section for City & Guilds awards in these areas.

Phonographic Performance Licence (PPL) and PRS for Music (formerly Performing Right Society)

When a sound recording is played in public, there are two separate licences that must be obtained. Under the Copyright Design and Patents Act 1988, there is a copyright in the musical and lyrical composition (PRS) and a separate copyright in the actual sound recording (PPL).

PRS represents the owners (ie the writer or composer) of the music and a PRS music licence grants legal permission to play the music on public premises.

PPL authorises any 'public' use of sound recording. 'Public' is considered to be any event except a family or domestic gathering. Playing music without a licence could result in court action.

For more information about the two types of licence, see www.prsformusic.com (PRS) and www.ppluk.com (PPL).

Gambling Act 2005

The Gambling Act 2005 came into effect on 1 September 2007 and is regulated by the Gambling Commission.

The Act is based on three licensing objectives. These are to:
- keep crime out of gambling
- ensure that gambling is conducted in a fair and open way
- protect children and vulnerable people from being harmed or exploited by gambling.

Under the Act, premises that are licensed to sell alcohol for consumption on the premises will be permitted to provide equal chance gaming (including poker and bingo) but are subject to strict conditions. These conditions include limits on stake money, prizes, fees and record keeping. It is advisable that you check with the LSO or Licensing Board before you allow any type of gaming or gambling on your premises. This includes traditional pub games such as cribbage and dominoes.

Amusement with Prize (AWP) machines are also strictly regulated. Alcohol licensed premises, except off-sales, are allowed two category 'C' or 'D' machines. They must notify the Licensing Board and pay a one-off fee of £50.

Certain lotteries, draws and sweepstakes are permissible, but there are conditions attached to the prizes and the destination of the profits: they must not be for commercial gain. Some must be registered.

All gaming, whether machines or games, must be run in accordance with the Gambling Commission's statutory code of practice. For more information, you can visit the Gambling Commissions's website: www.gamblingcommission.gov.uk

Relevant criminal legislation

Misuse of Drugs Act

This is the main piece of legislation covering drugs and categorises drugs as class 'A', 'B' and 'C'. These drugs are termed as controlled substances, and Class A drugs are those considered to be the most harmful.

Offences under the Act include:
- unlawful possession of a controlled substance
- possession of a controlled substance with intent to supply it
- supplying or offering to supply a controlled drug (even where no charge is made for the drug)
- allowing premises you occupy or manage to be used unlawfully for the purpose of producing or supplying controlled drugs.

Drug trafficking (supply) attracts serious punishment including life imprisonment for Class A offences. To enforce this law the police have special powers to stop, detain and search people on 'reasonable suspicion' that they are in possession of a controlled drug.

An Advisory Council on Misuse of Drugs was set up under the Act, which reviews the drug situation in the UK, and advises on misuse of drugs and related social problems. In 2007 it published a report on what is popularly known as 'date rape' – drugs facilitated sexual assault – including rapes in which drugs are mixed with alcohol. Handling drug-related issues on your premises is covered in Part 4. For further information, see http://drugs.homeoffice.gov.uk/drugs-laws/misuse-of-drugs-act.

Self check

1 What are the five steps involved in carrying out a risk assessment?

2 Which regulations cover the safety of food for human consumption?

3 Name three products that can only be sold to a person over the age of 16.

4 Name the two bodies responsible for advertising.

5 What is the difference between non-alcoholic and low-alcohol drinks?

6 What are the only measures that can be used to sell draught beer and cider?

7 Under the Disability Discrimination Act, what must licence holders do to accommodate disabled people?

8 Which council department enforces the smoking ban in public places in Scotland?

9 Under the SIA regulations, there are now two types of licence. What are they?

Test practice

1 Once a risk assessment has been completed, which one of the following should happen?

a It must be reviewed at regular intervals
b It should be stored in the safe
c Staff should attend a health and safety course
d It should be sent to the Health & Safety Executive

2 What are an employee's responsibilities under the Health and Safety at Work Act?

a To ensure that they inform their colleagues before doing something risky
b To ensure that there is a risk assessment for their working practices
c To ensure that their working practices maintain the health and safety of themselves and their colleagues
d To ensure that they have recorded their working practices in the health and safety manual

3 Which one of these is not illegal?

a To sell food that is past its 'use by' date
b To sell food that is past its 'best before' date
c To sell food that is unfit for human consumption
d To sell food that is falsely or misleadingly presented

4 Which one of these is included in the code of practice for advertising alcohol?

a Advertisements should be socially responsible
b Advertisements should encourage excessive drinking
c Advertisements should suggest alcohol can enhance mental, physical or sexual capabilities
d Drinking alcohol should be portrayed as a challenge

Alcohol – and its influences

Alcohol – and its influences

The recent changes to licensing legislation are one part of the Scottish Government's action to tackle Scotland's rising alcohol problems. In 2002 the first Plan for Action on Alcohol Problems was published and led to a review of licensing legislation. The Plan for Action was updated in 2007, and then in 2009 Changing Scotland's Relationship with Alcohol: A Framework for Action was published. In 2010 we saw some of the issues in the Framework becoming legislation - mainly through the Alcohol etc (Scotland) Act 2010. These changes are included in this Guidebook. The Government's current alcohol policy can be viewed on www.scotland.gov.uk.

This part of the book looks at what alcohol is and how it affects us. It explains how to calculate units, and sums up what experts have to say about 'safe' drinking habits. It outlines some of the common patterns of alcohol misuse in Scotland. Immediate problems that can result from acute intoxication, such as injuries and violence, are covered, as well as the longer term problems linked with continued excessive drinking, such as harm to physical and mental health.

What is alcohol?

Alcohol is a drug, that is, a substance that affects the way the brain (and body) functions. Alcohol is a legal drug, regulated by the Licensing (Scotland) Act 2005. Under the Act 'alcohol' means spirits, wines, beer, cider and any other fermented, distilled or spirituous liquor.

It does not include:
- alcohol 0.5% or less
- perfume
- any flavouring essence recognised by Customs and Excise as not being intended for consumption as or with dutiable alcoholic liquor
- the aromatic flavouring essence known as angostura bitters
- alcohol which is, or is included in, a medicinal product
- denatured alcohol
- methyl alcohol
- naphtha
- alcohol contained in liqueur confectionery.

Alcohol is our 'drug of choice'. In this country we have a culture of heavy drinking (too much overall) and binge drinking (too much at one time). Both tend to lead to drunkenness. Because alcohol is legal, many people see it as safe and tend to underestimate or be unaware of its effects. As servers of alcohol, with the legal responsibility to decide who you should and should not serve, it's particularly important that you're aware of all the effects of alcohol.

Alcohol and the brain

What kind of drug is alcohol? Is it a stimulant that 'peps' you up and makes your body go faster, or is it a depressant – one that slows you down? Many people are unsure about this. Alcohol is a depressant. This is because of the way that it works, especially on the brain.

One of the first areas of the brain to be 'numbed' is the area that controls judgement, emotions and inhibitions. This may make people seem more chatty or become the life and soul of the party. This is one of the effects that can make alcohol dangerous; it makes people feel unstoppable. It contributes to a number of accidents and deaths. People think they can do more than they actually can, such as swimming an unrealistic distance or driving a car at high speed.

In fact alcohol tends to worsen physical and mental functioning, so people are likely to be capable of less, not more, than usual. The illustration below shows the areas of the brain that become increasingly depressed as the alcohol level rises:

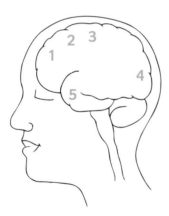

1 emotion centre – resulting in fewer inhibitions, person becoming more relaxed
2 speech centre – resulting in slurred speech
3 movement centre – resulting in unsteady movement
4 vision centre – resulting in difficulty in focusing or 'double vision'
5 primitive brain – this is the part that keeps a person alive, the heart beating and lungs working.

If the primitive brain is affected by excessive alcohol, a person is likely to become unconscious and this can be fatal. This is known as 'alcohol poisoning'. You and your staff must make sure that you never serve someone this much alcohol.

All staff need to watch for the signs that someone is becoming drunk. You should discuss with your staff at what point a customer will be judged to be drunk and will be refused service. Clear guidance should be included in your house or store policy. In dealing with a drunken person, it's important to keep in mind that they may be slower to understand than usual and quicker to anger. Ways of handling such situations are discussed more in Part 4 of this book.

Units of alcohol

When a person takes a drink of alcohol, its effects begin very quickly, generally within five minutes. As a person keeps drinking, the level of alcohol in the blood rises. If this continued unchecked, it could be fatal. The liver breaks down and neutralises the alcohol, processing it out of the body. This generally begins about twenty minutes after a person starts drinking. The liver works at a consistent rate of approximately one unit per hour (although this may be slower if the person is unwell). There is nothing that can be done to speed up this rate.

There are various myths about how to sober a person up:

Drinking coffee	Trying to sober up a drunken person by giving them large amounts of coffee is setting up a conflict of drugs. Coffee can even worsen the effect because it contains caffeine, which speeds up the body so that more alcohol is carried to the brain.
Drinking water	Drinking water will offset some of the dehydrating effects of alcohol. This in turn might prevent a person from having such a sore head in the morning, but it won't affect the amount of alcohol they've drunk.
Eating something	Eating before drinking will slow down the rate at which alcohol gets into the bloodstream. Eating after drinking will make no difference.
A good night's sleep	Sleeping does not make the liver process the alcohol out of your body any quicker. In fact, alcohol – even in very small amounts – disturbs normal sleep patterns.
Being sick	Being sick only gets rid of the alcohol that is still in the stomach. It does not affect the amount that has already been absorbed into the blood.

Did you know?

44% of men and 34% of women exceed recommended daily limits. (Scottish Health Survey 2009).

Units and 'drinks'

Being able to work out the units of alcohol in a drink gives a simple way to compare the amount of alcohol contained in one drink with another. It also allows a person to compare their drinking with sensible drinking limits. Understanding the number of units per drink also helps in calculating how long it will take all the alcohol to be broken down (which may not be until the following day!).

In Britain a unit is 10 ml of pure alcohol (8 grams of alcohol). This is sometimes said to be the equivalent to the alcohol contained in one 'drink'. The rest of the drink is water, flavouring and colourings.

However, the simple idea that one drink – for example, a glass of wine, a sherry, a nip or a half pint of beer or cider – equals one unit was introduced some time ago when people generally drank standard strength beers and lower strength German wines. Things are very different today. For instance the strength of beer ranges from low alcohol beer at about 1% ABV (alcohol by volume), to standard beer of about 3.5% ABV, or 4% in Scotland, through to super strength beers of around 8% ABV.

In order to find out the exact number of units in a drink you need to do a simple calculation. First multiply the volume of the drink in millilitres by the ABV, and then divide by 1000.

Formula	size (ml) × strength (ABV) ÷ 1000 = units
Example	750 ml bottle of wine at 13% ABV means (750 × 13) = 9750 9750 ÷ 1000 = 9.75 units

How much is too much?

The Royal College of Physicians in London has drawn up some guidelines to suggest what 'safe' limits of units of alcohol consumed in one week might be:

	Women	Men
Low risk	up to 14	up to 21
Increased danger	14–35	21–49
Dangerous	over 35	over 49

When these guidelines came out, people tended to 'save' their units and drink them all in one session of 'binge drinking'. As this was not a 'safe' way of drinking, in 1995 a government report suggested that weekly limits should be revised to daily limits.

The report by the Department of Health suggested that men who drink three to four units a day (but not more) and women who drink two to three units per day (but not more) don't face a significant health risk. There should also be at least two alcohol-free days each week.

Don't forget that an average glass of wine in a pub (250 ml at 13% ABV) and a pint of premium lager at 5% ABV are each equivalent to around three units. Consistently drinking more than this in one day is not advisable because of the increased health risk.

As public ideas about the number of units in a drink are generally outdated, confusion continues over 'safe' levels of different kinds of drinks. Knowing how to calculate units of alcohol helps in making comparisons. If a female wished to keep within the safe daily limits of two to three units on a night out, she could either have one large glass of wine, or two bottles of alcopops or three vodka and cokes.

Children and young people

As with any drug, a person who drinks alcohol regularly will develop a certain tolerance to it. This doesn't mean that they become immune to alcohol, but only that it takes more alcohol before it appears that they are affected.

For young people drinking alcohol can be problematic not only because they are smaller, which means they will have a higher concentration of alcohol in the blood than adults, but also because they are just beginning to use alcohol, and so will have lower tolerance: even a single unit of alcohol may have a large effect. This means that they can reach the level of acute alcohol poisoning – which can be fatal – with far less alcohol than an adult who drinks regularly.

Remember, even though a young person has reached their adult height, their internal organs may not be fully developed and are therefore more susceptible to damage from small amounts of alcohol. For young people whose bodies have matured, drinking alcohol in itself is not necessarily harmful, but drinking too much, too quickly and in hazardous situations can be dangerous.

A young person may be less psychologically mature, so may not act responsibly and this, coupled with the effect of alcohol (the suppression of inhibition and the increased tendency to take risks), means that they have a greater likelihood of accidents, getting involved in a fight or getting into a risky situation.

There has been a worrying increase in the number of young people drinking alcohol, with an increase of 54% in the number of 15 year olds and a 100% increase in the number of 13 years olds drinking in the last decade. Scottish school children are asked to take part in the biennial Scottish Schools Adolescent Lifestyle and Substance Use Survey (SALSUS). In the 2008 survey 82% of 15 year olds said they had had an alcoholic drink, along with 52% of 13 year olds. Those who had drunk alcohol were asked if they had experienced outcomes ranging from vomiting to being admitted to hospital. The effects of drinking are shown in the table on page 61.

Where do young people purchase alcohol?

Although it is illegal to sell alcohol to under-18s, we know that some licensees do. In evidence given to the Nicholson Committee, young consultees (ie under-18s) confirmed that some, though by no means all, small licensed grocers or corner shops tend to be favoured places for purchasing alcohol 'without any questions being asked'. In the 2006 SALSUS survey, a majority of 13 year olds who had drunk alcohol said that they didn't buy it, and nearly 40% of 15 year olds said the same. Presumably they were given alcohol by friends or family. Of 15 year olds who did buy alcohol, 19% said they'd purchased it from an off-licence, 7% from a supermarket and 7% from a pub. The sources of purchased alcohol are shown in the table on page 61.

What will young people try to buy?

In 2006 Alcohol Focus Scotland carried out a study of refusals books from a range of premises throughout Scotland over a five month period. The results are shown in the table on page 62. The most popular purchases were vodka and lager. Why? If young people drink alcohol to make them feel more 'grown up', it makes sense that they will mimic adult behaviour. The products most commonly consumed by adults are vodka and lager.

Effects of alcohol on young people

☺ ☺ ☺ ☺ ☺ ☺ ☺ ☺ ☺ ☺ ☺ ☺	39%	vomited
☺ ☺ ☺ ☺ ☺ ☺ ☺ ☺ ☺ ☺ ☺ ☺	39%	had an argument
☺ ☺ ☺ ☺ ☺ ☺ ☺ ☺ ☺	23%	been in trouble with police
☺ ☺ ☺ ☺ ☺ ☺ ☺	19%	had a fight
☺ ☺ ☺ ☺ ☺ ☺	18%	tried drugs
☺ ☺ ☺ ☺ ☺	12%	taken home by police
☺ ☺ ☺ ☺	10%	stayed off school
☺ ☺ ☺	6%	had an injury seen by doctor
☺ ☺	5%	visited A&E
☺	3%	admitted to hospital

0%   25%   50%   75%   100%

Where do young people get alcohol?

☺ ☺ ☺ ☺ ☺ ☺ ☺ ☺ ☺ ☺ ☺ ☺	38%	never buy alcohol
☺ ☺ ☺ ☺ ☺ ☺ ☺ ☺ ☺ ☺	32%	friend or relative
☺ ☺ ☺ ☺ ☺ ☺	19%	shop
☺ ☺ ☺ ☺ ☺ ☺	16%	off-licence
☺ ☺ ☺	6%	supermarket
☺ ☺	4%	pub
☺	3%	someone else
☺	3%	club or disco

0%   25%   50%   75%   100%

The graph at the top shows the effects of drinking experienced by 15 year olds at least once in the last year.

The graph at the bottom shows sources for 15 year olds who said they had drunk alcohol.

Percentages of both graphs add up to more than 100% because the 15 year olds were given a list of options and asked to pick all that apply.

Source: SALSUS, 2008 report.

There is also another group of products that are more about 'bang for buck', that is maximum strength for minimum cost, such as large bottles of high strength cider. These are the next most popular purchases. There were some local variations – for example, in some areas young people drink perry (eg Lambrini).

It's a requirement that you train your staff, so make sure your training includes the very good reasons why the legal age to purchase alcohol has been set at 18. They also need to know what young people try to buy. It's up to you and your staff to enforce the law. Information on how to deal with refusal of service is covered in Part 4 of this book.

What do young people try to buy?

vodka	23%
lager	17%
tonic wine	15%
cider	12%
alcopop	10%
wine	9%

0%　　　25%　　　50%　　　75%　　　100%

Drink driving, accidents and crime

Drinking and driving

In 2009/2010 there were over 8,500 drink driving offences in Scotland and in 2007 460 deaths in the UK were caused by people over the drink/drive limit. With this in mind, is there a safe limit for drinking and driving? Most experts would definitely say no!

The legal alcohol limit for driving in the UK is currently 80 milligrams of alcohol in 100 millilitres of blood which equates to 35 micrograms of alcohol in 100 millilitres of breath. It would be extremely difficult to identify how many drinks it will take for someone to reach the legal limit, because it is dependent on a number of factors.

Gender	Women (like it or not) have more fat and less water in their bodies, and are generally smaller, which gives less volume to dilute the alcohol.
Physical size	A larger person has a larger volume and more water in which to dilute the alcohol.
Other factors	Whether the person has eaten recently, whether they are in good health, etc.
Type of drink	Fizzy alcoholic drinks, such as sparkling wine or cider, and stronger drinks, like spirits, tend to be absorbed more quickly.

Is the legal limit safe?

The present drink driving limit in the UK is 80 mg alcohol/100 ml of blood, but impairment occurs well before this stage:

20–50 mg	Ability to see moving lights and judge distances is diminished.
50–80 mg	Ability to judge distances is definitely impaired, adaptability of eyes to changing light is impaired, reactions and concentration span are shorter.
80 mg	**Legal limit**
80–120 mg	Exhilaration sets in, leading to overestimation of own driving abilities, which can cause reckless driving. Peripheral vision (out of the corner of the eye) and the ability to assess dimensions are impaired.
120 mg	Driver is ten times more likely to have an accident than if there was no alcohol in their blood.

Graph at the top from Alcohol Focus Scotland, 2006.

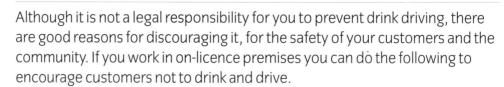

Although it is not a legal responsibility for you to prevent drink driving, there are good reasons for discouraging it, for the safety of your customers and the community. If you work in on-licence premises you can do the following to encourage customers not to drink and drive.

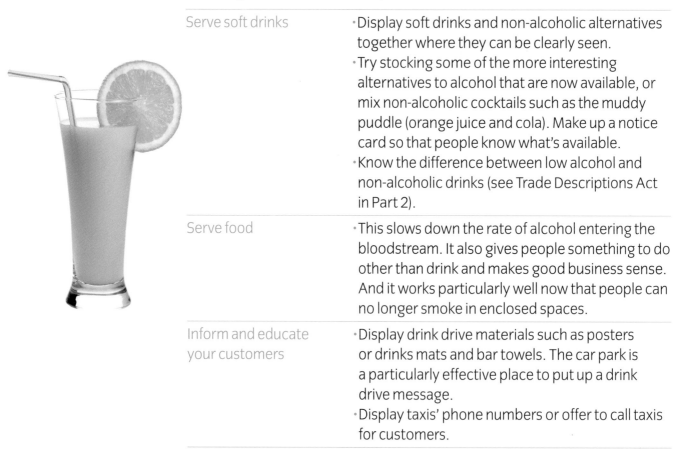

Serve soft drinks	• Display soft drinks and non-alcoholic alternatives together where they can be clearly seen. • Try stocking some of the more interesting alternatives to alcohol that are now available, or mix non-alcoholic cocktails such as the muddy puddle (orange juice and cola). Make up a notice card so that people know what's available. • Know the difference between low alcohol and non-alcoholic drinks (see Trade Descriptions Act in Part 2).
Serve food	• This slows down the rate of alcohol entering the bloodstream. It also gives people something to do other than drink and makes good business sense. And it works particularly well now that people can no longer smoke in enclosed spaces.
Inform and educate your customers	• Display drink drive materials such as posters or drinks mats and bar towels. The car park is a particularly effective place to put up a drink drive message. • Display taxis' phone numbers or offer to call taxis for customers.

A few words of caution: don't exceed your authority. If someone is clearly over the limit and you realise they're intending to drive, you could offer to call them a taxi, but you cannot take their keys from them unless they choose to hand them over. This could be seen as theft. Don't try to physically restrain a person as this could be seen as assault. You may feel it's friendly to offer to drive someone home, but if you have an accident you could face insurance problems. An option is to phone the police anonymously on Crimestoppers 0800 555 111. Your house policy should include your policy on drinking drivers.

Costs to Scotland of alcohol misuse

In 2006–07, a total of £2.25 billion:
· NHS – £405 million
· Social work – £170 million
· Criminal Justice and Emergency Services – £385 million
· Wider economic costs – £820 million
· Human costs – £470 million.

This equates to over £500 per year for every adult living in Scotland.

The social consequences

· 40% of male and 31% of female prisoners, and 66% of younger offenders, reported being drunk at the time of committing their offence. Information Service Division, NHS National Services, Scotland 2007.
· In 46% of all violent incidents, 58% of stranger violence, 47% of acquaintance violence and 39% of domestic violence, offenders are considered to be under the influence of alcohol. British Crime Survey 2006.
· 62% of murders in Glasgow were committed in the victim's own home (often by friends and relatives with whom they were drinking). Scottish Government, Homicide in Scotland 2002.
· 19% of violent crimes take place in and around pubs and clubs. Nicholson committee Report 2003.
· 70% of all assaults who attend emergency departments are alcohol related. Scottish Emergency Department Alcohol Audit 2006.
· 1 in 3 divorce petitions in the UK cite excessive drinking by a partner as a contributory factor. Alcohol Harm Reduction project: Interim Analytical Report, Prime Minister's Strategy Unit, 2003.
· Children whose parents drink at problematical levels have been found to have higher levels of behavioural difficulty, school-related problems and emotional disturbance. Looking Beyond Risk: Parental Substance Misuse: Scoping Study, Scottish Executive, 2006.

The figures at the top are from the Scottish Government's 'Changing Scotland's Relationship with Alcohol' paper, www.scotland.gov.uk/Publications/2008/06/16084348/0.

Fire

Fire and Rescue Service figures show that in 2006–07, twenty people lost their lives in alcohol-related fires in Scotland. In 2005–06, 58% of all fire fatalities in Strathclyde were directly related to alcohol abuse. The most common causes of fires where alcohol is a contributory factor involve the careless use of cigarettes, lighters and matches, or misuse of chip pans and cooking appliances while making food. A new campaign was launched in 2006 to raise awareness of the direct link between alcohol misuse and accidental fires.

Accident and emergency

Did you know?

1 in 9 people (11%) attending Accident and Emergency has alcohol-related injuries. This rises to eight out of ten at peak times.

Unfortunately alcohol is involved in many more accidents, injuries and fatalities than we commonly realise. It is the police and medical staff who have to cope with the results. The Scottish Government has calculated the cost of alcohol misuse to Criminal Justice and the Emergency Services at £385 million in 2006–07. For other costs, see page 65. The peak time for accidents and injuries falls just after the majority of licensed premises close. The high points are Friday and Saturday nights between midnight and 04.00. Pubs tend to close at 23.00 or midnight, and clubs between 01.00 and 03.00. There are approximately 400 alcohol related deaths from home accidents annually in the UK (Source www.ias.org.uk).

It's worth considering what happens to persons found by the police to be 'drunk and incapable' (which is actually an offence). Are they left lying in the street? Are they sent home alone? No. They're either taken to hospital to be checked and then kept in the police cells where someone can keep an eye on them or taken to an alcohol detoxification centre, again where they will be supervised.

Drunk and incapable persons are detained because they pose such a risk to themselves and others. It is with good reason that the laws on drunkenness exist. It's up to you and your staff to enforce them.

Crime

Drunkenness has a high association with some common crimes (see figures on page 65). People who are drunk:
- are more likely to assault someone or be assaulted (particularly young men)
- have a higher likelihood of being involved in domestic violence, such as assaulting their partner or their children.

The law gives you and your staff a legal responsibility to decide whether to continue to sell alcohol or to refuse. Customers, particularly those who have already been drinking, may not be in the best position to judge for themselves. If you work in an off-sales premises, you don't know when or where a customer is going to consume the alcohol being purchased, but it is likely that a drunk person is buying more alcohol to consume immediately.

Health

Both health professionals and the government are concerned about the risks to health associated with drinking large quantities of alcohol. In 2005 there were 2,372 deaths involving alcohol as an 'underlying' or 'contributory' factor. Males accounted for almost two thirds of these deaths, and females just over one third. According to a 2009 NHS report, it is estimated that one Scot dies every 3 hours as a direct result of alcohol misuse.

Alcohol problems take many different forms, including binge drinking, 'needing' a drink (eg to relax) and drinking above sensible limits.

Health threats

There are many ways in which alcohol can put health at risk. Short-term health problems, associated with binge drinking, include:
- hangover (headache, nausea, etc)
- temporary memory loss
- disturbed sleep patterns
- increased risk of stroke and heart problems
- high blood pressure
- impotency
- accidents and injuries
- acute alcohol poisoning
- unwanted and/or unprotected sex and associated risk of pregnancy and sexually transmitted infections.

Long-term excessive consumption of alcohol can lead to problems in a number of areas, including finance, relationships and employment, as well as health.

Pregnancy
Pregnant women or women trying to conceive should avoid drinking alcohol. Although researchers don't know exactly how much alcohol is safe to drink when pregnant, we do know that the risk of damage to the unborn baby increases the more alcohol is consumed. Binge drinking is particularly harmful.

If pregnant women do choose to drink, they should not drink more than one to two units of alcohol once or twice a week and should not get drunk, in order to minimise the risk to the baby. Heavy drinking is associated with miscarriage, and sometimes with serious effects on a baby's development including:

- premature birth
- low birth weight
- facial deformity
- hearing and vision problems
- growth deficits
- motor skills problems
- hyperactivity
- memory, attention and judgment problems
- language problems
- difficulties at school.

Brain damage and intellectual impairment

Heavy drinkers show brain shrinkage on brain scans. In addition there are a number of brain-related illnesses associated with people who overuse alcohol over long periods of time. Unfortunately these conditions are on the increase.

Liver-related problems

Alcohol is primarily broken down in the liver, which can damage the liver cells. Very small amounts are also excreted in the breath and sweat. As the alcohol is broken down, calories are released, which if not 'burnt up' become fat. This fat can be stored in the liver: a 'fatty liver' is the first stage of liver problems. The liver is swollen and tender. This is reversible if drinking stops or reduces. Cirrhosis occurs when liver cells die leaving scarring or distortion of the liver. People can live with a degree of cirrhosis if they stop drinking.

In most cases liver disease is a chronic condition that has built up over time. It is most commonly a disease that affects people who have been drinking hazardously over a number of years. The highest rates of cirrhosis tend to be found in people in their late 40s or their 50s. However, in recent years cirrhosis rates in younger age groups have also increased. The chart on page 69 gives a comparison of deaths attributed to cirrhoses of the liver in Scotland, England and Wales, and other European countries.

Some people with cirrhosis will go on to develop hepatitis and/or cancer of the liver. Without a transplant, this tends to be fatal as the liver is one of those essential organs that we cannot function without.

Deaths attributed to liver disease

In 1990, one in 100 deaths was directly attributed to alcohol. The NHS report, 'Alcohol attributable mortality and morbidity' published in 2009, showed this had risen to 1 in 20 deaths in less than 20 years. This rise compares very badly to the rest of Europe. The table below charts deaths from chronic liver disease and cirrhosis of the liver in Scotland, England and Wales, and other European countries.

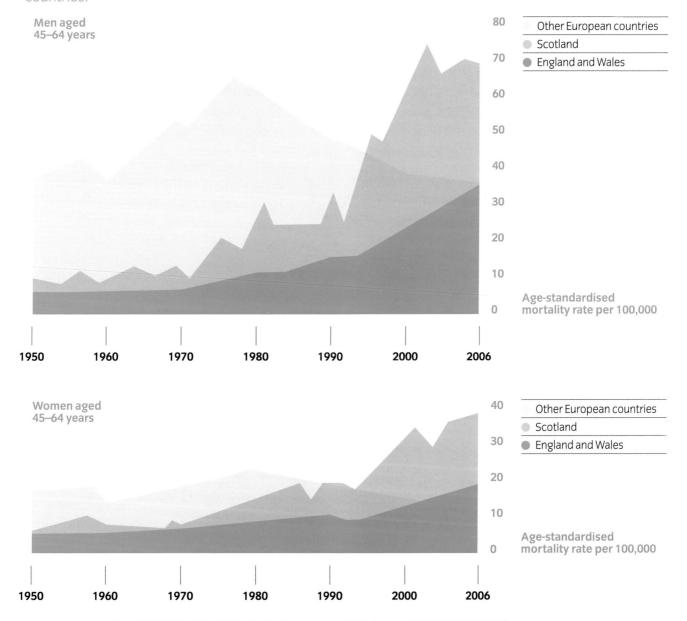

Men aged 45–64 years

Other European countries
Scotland
England and Wales

Age-standardised mortality rate per 100,000

1950   1960   1970   1980   1990   2000   2006

Women aged 45–64 years

Other European countries
Scotland
England and Wales

Age-standardised mortality rate per 100,000

1950   1960   1970   1980   1990   2000   2006

Graphs based on 'Liver cirrhosis mortality rates in Britain from 1950 to 2002: an analysis of routine data', *The Lancet*, Vol. 367, January 2007. Rates for England and Wales (to 2004) and Scotland (to 2006) subsequently updated by Professor David Leon and the General Registrar for Scotland.

Cancers

As well as cancer of the liver, heavy drinkers seem more susceptible to certain other cancers than 'social' drinkers. If a person is also a smoker this again increases the probability of getting cancer. Cancers that are thought to have an increased incidence in heavy drinkers include: liver, esophageal (gullet), head and neck cancers (including mouth and throat) and breast cancer. Remember that all these can occur without heavy drinking.

Pancreatitis

The pancreas is responsible for producing digestive enzymes and insulin. Pancreatitis can be acute or chronic. Alcohol is the second most common cause of acute pancreatitis, the symptoms of which include severe central abdominal pain, loss of appetite, diarrhoea and weight loss. Chronic pancreatitis is caused by drinking alcohol to excess over a long period of time. If the pancreas cannot fulfil its function of producing insulin as a result of pancreatitis, the person will experience problems related to diabetes.

However, the vast majority of diabetes conditions are not caused by heavy drinking. Yet if someone is diagnosed as diabetic for whatever reason, they do have to take into account the high number of calories in alcoholic drinks.

Cardiac problems

There is some evidence that light drinking (less than two to three units per day for women and less than three to four units for men) has a beneficial effect on the heart. However, this beneficial effect is only been shown to apply to men over 40 and post-menopausal women.

Heavy drinking can result in heart damage. The heart muscle can enlarge and become less efficient at its job of pumping blood around the body, contributing to cardiomyopathy and congestive heart failure.

Blood pressure

Drinking causes fluctuations in blood pressure. Alcohol causes blood vessels to dilate (open up wider) resulting in a temporary drop in blood pressure. However, there is an established link between high blood pressure and alcohol intake. Regular heavy drinking, and particularly binge drinking, is associated with raising blood pressure which puts the individual at risk of a stroke. High doses of alcohol can result in the blood being more likely to clot. A bout of heavy drinking is one of the most common reasons for strokes in young people.

It's also important to remember that high blood pressure and strokes can occur for a number of other reasons and sometimes no known reason.

Gastritis

Nausea and vomiting, sometimes with blood, are not uncommon. Alcohol can irritate the lining of the stomach. Chronic gastritis can reduce the appetite resulting in vitamin deficiencies.

Fertility

Both men and women can be affected. In men, excessive drinking can lower sperm count, be a factor in impotence and can cause hormonal imbalances that result in testicular shrinkage and breast development. In women, the ovaries can decrease in size and a reduction in the hormone oestrogen can result in smaller breasts and male hair distribution. Heavy drinking is thought to increase the chances of spontaneous abortion (miscarriage).

Skin conditions

Alcohol is a dehydrant – it takes water away from the body. If the skin is continually dehydrated, it will become grey and dry looking.

High-risk occupations

If you work in an on-licence premises, you should be aware that you're in a high-risk occupation for cirrhosis of the liver and other diseases associated with alcohol. The graphs on page 73, based on figures for England and Wales, show that bar staff are the most likely workers to die of alcohol-related problems, with bar managers coming close behind. Indications are that risks are equally high in Scotland.

Why are some occupations high-risk? Three main factors tend to increase risk:
- alcohol is easily available
- alcohol is at an affordable price
- the occupation is stressful.

Bear in mind that just because in your lifestyle you 'normally' spend a lot of time in a pub and may also socialise there, this may not be 'normal' for everyone. Licensees may have to pay higher rates of insurance because of their increased risk.

You should also consider the possible effects of alcohol misuse on your business. Staff members with an alcohol problem are likely to have periods when they are not functioning well, and also increased periods of absence. Do what you can to reduce any risks and have in a place a policy to deal with problems, if they arise.

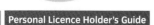

Some things you can do:
- make sure you run any staff social events responsibly
- train your staff to understand the risks alcohol poses to their own health
- have in place an alcohol policy that states your rules on staff drinking while at work and how you would support someone with an alcohol problem. For more help in creating an alcohol policy, seek the guidance of a specialist agency such as Alcohol Focus Scotland.

Health and the Licensing Act

The effect of alcohol misuse on Scotland's health is huge and rapidly growing worse. This is why the Licensing (Scotland) Act 2005 includes a licensing objective on health. Licensees may be required to set out in their operating plan how they intend to meet the five licensing objectives, one of which is protecting and improving public health. You may want to consider the following suggestions:

On-licence	- promote competitively priced non-alcoholic drinks - encourage customers to eat as well as drink - use smaller measures for wine and spirits - encourage customers to space out alcoholic drinks with soft drinks - don't allow customers to play drinking games - limit the number of drinks that can be purchased, ie one drink per person - avoid time limited promotions.
Off-licence	- promote quality over quantity - avoid promotions that offer multiple purchases - limit the amount of alcohol to be purchased.
Both on- and off-licence	- display information on units of alcohol and the dangers of excessive drinking - offer drinks with a lower alcoholic strength - train staff on the effects of alcohol - promote alternatives to alcohol.

Try the 'Promoting sensible drinking' checklist in the 'More information' section at the end of this book.

Risk of alcohol-related death by occupation (male)

☺☺☺☺☺☺☺☺☺☺☺☺☺☺☺☺☺☺☺☺☺☺☺☺☺☺☺☺☺☺☺☺☺☺☺☺						Bar staff
☺☺☺☺☺☺☺☺☺☺☺☺☺☺☺☺☺☺☺☺☺☺☺☺☺☺☺☺☺☺☺☺☺						Seafarers
☺☺☺☺☺☺☺☺☺☺☺☺☺☺☺☺☺☺☺☺☺☺☺☺☺☺☺☺☺☺						Landlords & bar managers
☺☺☺☺☺☺☺☺☺☺☺☺☺☺☺☺☺☺☺☺☺☺☺☺☺☺						Senior civil servants
☺☺☺☺☺☺☺☺☺☺☺☺☺☺☺☺☺☺☺☺☺☺						Security guards
☺☺☺☺☺☺☺						Construction managers
☺☺☺☺☺☺☺						Driving instructors
☺☺☺☺☺☺						Clergy
☺☺☺☺☺☺						IT managers
☺☺☺☺☺						Farmers

| 0 | 0.5 | Average | 1.5 | 2.0 | 2.5 | Death rates |

Risk of alcohol-related death by occupation (female)

☺☺☺☺☺☺☺☺☺☺☺☺☺☺☺☺☺☺☺☺☺☺☺☺☺☺☺☺☺☺☺						Bar staff
☺☺☺☺☺☺☺☺☺☺☺☺☺☺☺☺☺☺☺☺☺☺☺☺☺☺☺☺☺						Landlords & bar managers
☺☺☺☺☺☺☺☺☺☺☺☺☺☺☺☺☺☺☺☺☺☺☺☺☺☺☺☺						Elementary office staff
☺☺☺☺☺☺☺☺☺☺☺☺☺☺☺☺☺☺☺☺☺☺☺☺☺						Actors/entertainers
☺☺☺☺☺☺☺☺☺☺☺☺☺☺☺☺☺☺☺☺☺						Waitresses
☺☺☺☺☺☺☺☺						Managers
☺☺☺☺☺☺☺☺						Nursery nurses
☺☺☺☺☺☺☺☺						Childminders
☺☺☺☺☺☺						School midday assistants
☺☺☺☺☺						Educational assistants

| 0 | 0.5 | Average | 1.5 | 2.0 | 2.5 | Death rates |

Figures for England and Wales, 2001–05. Source: Office of National Statistics

What to do if a person collapses

Sometimes it may be difficult to tell whether a person is intoxicated by alcohol (or another drug) or whether they have some form of illness or disability. If the person collapses, your response should be the same:

1 call for help immediately
2 call an ambulance (or ask someone to do it for you)
3 check that their airways are clear
4 check if the person is breathing or not
5 loosen any tight clothing, especially at the neck and waist.

If the person is breathing, put them into the recovery position and stay with them until help arrives. The opposite page gives basic advice on opening the airway and the recovery position. This is not a substitute for training. For information on first aid courses, contact the local branch of the Red Cross (www.redcross.org.uk) or St Andrew's Ambulance Association (www.firstaid.org.uk).

Monitoring

If the person has not collapsed but is showing signs of intoxication or other suspicious behaviour, they need to be monitored until you can decide what action is appropriate. Watch them carefully from a distance, or ask staff to keep an eye on them; perhaps try talking with them. Do not throw the person alone onto the street. This would be both dangerous and irresponsible.

National campaigns and strategies

There are many initiatives promoting safe and responsible drinking and lots of information is available. Alcohol Focus Scotland offers a range of literature downloadable from its website: www.alcohol-focus-scotland.org.uk.

Scottish Government

The Scottish Government and NHS Health Scotland have funded a number of campaigns challenging the Scottish attitude to drinking. Information is available in the alcohol section in 'Healthier Scotland' of the website www.infoscotland.com. The Scottish Government's alcohol policy documents are available at www.scotland.gov.uk.

The latest alcohol and health statistics can be found at www.isdscotland.org.

Opening the airway

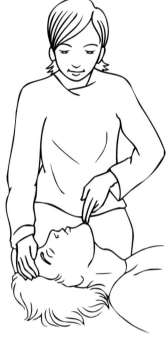

To open the airway:
1 place your hand on the person's forehead and gently tilt the head back
2 lift the chin with two fingertips.

The recovery position

Lie the person on their side and support them by bending their other leg. The arms should be bent to support their head, making sure the airway remains clear.

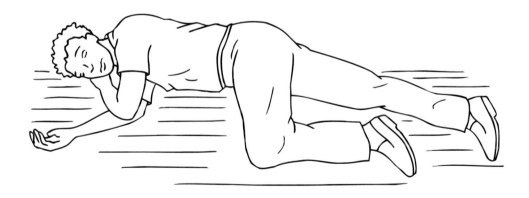

Alcohol and Drugs Partnerships (ADPs)

There are 30 Alcohol and Drugs Partnerships (ADPs) in Scotland which have been operational since October 2009. ADPs are responsible for developing and overseeing local strategies for tackling alcohol and drugs that are based on:

- an assessment of needs in the area;
- an evidence based process for agreeing how funds should be deployed, and;
- a clear focus on the outcomes that the investment will achieve in their community.

The strategies ensure all relevant partners play their part and better identify local needs.

In addition to working with treatment and care services for those with substance misuse problems, ADPs work with those delivering prevention and education. ADPs are embedded in wider community planning frameworks in each area, eg Community Planning Partnerships. They will also link to licensing structures - normally through membership of the Local Licensing Forum.

Self check

1 Name three types of alcohol covered by the Licensing (Scotland) Act 2005.

2 What type of drug is alcohol?

3 What are considered the safe weekly limits of alcohol for men and women?

4 How can you calculate what a unit of alcohol is?

5 What is the current drink driving limit?

6 Name three possible risks to health associated with drinking large quantities of alcohol.

7 Name two ways you can promote sensible drinking on your premises.

Test practice

1 Which of the following are possible consequences to an individual of excessive drinking on one occasion?

1 Increased risk of becoming a victim of crime
2 Increased risk of becoming successful
3 Death from alcohol poisoning
4 Short-term memory loss
5 Death from liver cirrhosis

a 1, 3, 4
b 1, 2, 5
c 1, 3, 5
d 2, 4, 3

2 Approximately how long will it take for alcohol to reach the liver?

a 2 minutes
b 20 minutes
c 2 hours
d 20 hours

3 Which one of the following best describes why binge drinking is a problem?

a People enjoy themselves too much
b People spend too much money
c People are more vulnerable to accidents
d People are more likely to be tired

4 If a unit of alcohol is 10 ml, which one of the following makes up the rest of every type of alcoholic drink?

a Water and sugar
b Caffeine and sugar
c Water and flavourings
d Caffeine and flavourings

4

The premises environment

As a premises or personal licence holder, you have responsibilities relating directly to the type of environment you create and the way you manage it. The Licensing (Scotland) Act 2005 requires you at all times to uphold the licensing objectives:

1 preventing crime and disorder

2 securing public safety

3 preventing public nuisance

4 protecting and improving public health

5 protecting children from harm.

This chapter looks at ways to help you create the right environment – one that is in keeping with the licensing objectives and one where customers have a high-quality experience and return to your premises again and again. The following information can help you fulfil your legal and social responsibilities and run a successful business.

The key aspects covered in this section are:

- offering good customer service
- creating the right setting
- preventing problems and dealing with situations promptly.

Did you know?

A typical dissatisfied customer will tell six to ten people about the problem. A typical satisfied customer will tell only one or two. Based on the National Complaints Culture Survey 2006, carried out by the National Association of Corporate Directors.

Customer service

Good customer service means having high standards in the way you treat customers. This includes being friendly, polite and helpful and being easily recognisable (ie wearing a uniform). It's not always easy to give good service, especially when you're busy, but it's important to do your best. The service that you and your staff give tends to be what stays in customers' minds after they have left. If they feel like they've had excellent service, they are more likely to come back. The reputation of your premises will often be based on the service customers receive. In turn, this means that customers know what to expect in your premises and it encourages them to behave to the same standards.

Working in a licensed premises, you have different roles to juggle. Two of the most important are 'salesperson' and 'police officer'. Good customer service requires that you and your staff are good at both.

The 'salesperson'

Selling is an important part of serving. If you didn't sell anything, you wouldn't have a business and your staff wouldn't have jobs. Train staff to:

- know the products that you sell. They need to know about your products as well as noting their ABV. You or your staff should be able to suggest an alternative if you don't have a particular drink so that you don't lose a sale.
- listen and learn. By listening to your customer and asking questions, you can find out exactly what the customer wants and make them feel valued.
- offer complementary products. Selling a wider range of products and recommending products that complement each other encourages customers to buy more and feel like they've received good service. For example, in an on-licence premises, selling food, coffee and other non-alcoholic drinks brings in more money. These items often have a higher profit margin than alcoholic drinks, and they give customers a choice. In an off-licence premises, selling related products, like crisps or snacks for people to enjoy with their drink, will benefit your bottom line.

The 'police officer'

The role of 'police officer', that is the enforcer of the law, is one that everyone – from new staff to experienced managers – generally feels less confident about. Providing good service can assist you with this role. By showing that you notice what happens, you put out the message that you're in control. Providing good service each time you come into contact with the customer reinforces this image. It also gives the impression that you and your staff are nice people who deserve respect. This means that people are more likely to be better behaved and your premises are less likely to be seen as a soft option for people wanting to carry out illegal activities, such as underage drinking or theft. It is also extremely important that there is communication between staff and that there are plans for what to do in difficult or conflict situations (an 'escalation policy') so that everyone works together.

It's best practice to establish a good relationship from the beginning. Make eye contact and welcome everyone who comes into the premises. If customers are ignored at this stage, it's more difficult to control them if they start to get disorderly or angry later. And remember, it is an offence for licence holders or staff to allow disorderly conduct.

Try the 'Customer service' checklist in the 'More information' section to see if there are areas where you could improve.

The right setting

Housekeeping

The things that annoy all customers seem to revolve around standards of basic cleanliness and housekeeping. Customers form an impression of your premises almost immediately when they come through the door (or even before – bright external lighting is welcoming but if the exterior is dirty and poorly maintained they may not bother coming in at all).

You need to ensure that the premises are in a good state of repair and that tidiness and cleanliness of the premises are maintained throughout the day. Other things that influence your customers are lighting, layout, decor, music, point-of-sale materials, other customers and staff – especially how quickly the staff notice them. If the counter is dirty or cluttered and the service poor, then it seems as if no-one will care about standards of behaviour either. The standards set by your premises will, to a large extent, determine the type of customers that you attract and their standards of behaviour.

Influencing behaviour

The relationship between alcohol and conflict is not a simple one. As we already know, one of the first effects of alcohol is to reduce inhibitions. If someone has been drinking and they become angry, they're less likely to be inhibited about what they say and do than they normally would be. We can't say that alcohol causes conflict; however, research carried out in on-licence premises suggests that conflict is more common where there is drunkenness.

Drinking behaviour depends on three different factors:

Alcohol	Amount of alcohol consumed on the occasion.
Person	Characteristics of the person drinking and that person's state of mind.
Environment	Atmosphere and rules of the establishment where the person is.

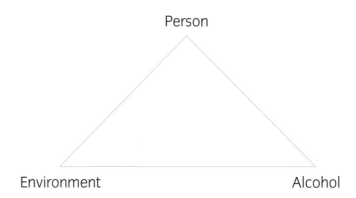

Changing any one of these factors will alter drinking behaviour. For example, a person's behaviour when sitting at home watching TV is likely to be very different from that same person's behaviour at a party or nightclub, where there are lots of people, loud music and movement, even if exactly the same amount of alcohol is consumed in both circumstances.

The manager and staff are in a position to control or influence at least two of these factors: the amount and type of drink served, and, in particular, the environment. The layout of the premises (whether there are more people sitting or standing, the lighting and the music) is something that you can influence. It's important that licensed premises strive for the kind of environment that encourages sensible drinking behaviour and discourages excessive drinking.

New licence holder or staff

Research has shown what people in the trade have always known: there is normally a 'run-in' period for new licence holders while they establish their own way of working in order to gain the behaviour expected from staff and customers. New staff, or staff newly having to deputise for the manager, as well as new licence holders, can experience a 'run-in' period. In order to minimise problems during this time, it's important that the new person understands the rules (such as the premises policies) and tries to keep the customers to these rules firmly and fairly.

Music

You may be providing music to attract customers or to influence them in some way. The type of music played and how loud it is can affect the behaviour of your customers. There have been some experiments with different types and speeds of music. In shops, playing classical music seems to reduce shoplifting. In bars, playing happy music at the end of the night can mean customers leave in a good mood.

Things for you to consider:
- What are your customers looking for? Is quiet background music appropriate or does it need to be the latest hits?
- How loud is it? Keep a check on volume and adjust to suit. Remember also that noise levels are restricted by health and safety regulations.

It's good practice to have a music policy, with different sorts of music for different times. The music can help to calm things down or liven things up as needed. It's not a good idea to save the best for last, when you are trying to get people to leave.

Problem customers

Your customers also have an effect on the atmosphere. Like tends to attract like, eg young people are likely to attract other young people, large groups attract other large groups and drunkenness attracts others who wish to behave in a rowdy manner. The same applies with the other 'problem groups', particularly in on-licence premises, such as people selling stolen goods and especially drug takers and dealers. It's much easier to prevent any sort of problem by taking action in the early stages, rather than trying to cure the problem later.

You must ensure you assess the risks in your premises, taking into account your customers and their likely behaviour. You should have policies and plans in place to prevent and manage situations.

Failure to do this could result in:
- your premises getting a bad reputation
- increased risk of arguments or conflict
- you being charged or fined, and your premises having its hours restricted or even losing its licence.

Tips for on-licence premises

Layout

We know that customers are going to move to certain areas. Most will visit the bar and inevitably also the toilets, as well as the main door in or out of the premises. If space is restricted in these areas, jostling among customers can easily lead to frustration and perhaps conflict. To avoid this, it is important to keep access to these areas as clear as possible.

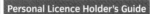

You may wish to consider:
- keeping tables, barstools or other obstructions away from these busy areas
- ensuring good access for staff – ie providing ways to get out from behind the bar/till point quickly to calm things down before trouble can start.

The layout can also affect the way that people are likely to behave. For instance, there is evidence to suggest that vertical drinking (ie where people stand) promotes more rapid drinking than when people are seated. The environment that you set can influence whether the customer is more likely to drink in a relaxed, social way or in an aggressive, competitive way.

Noise control
Make sure you consider the effects any noise from your premises could have on your neighbours. For example, if your bar is in an area where people live nearby, try to reduce the likelihood of noise disturbance by keeping the windows and doors closed. If you have a beer garden or external smoking area, be aware of any noise, mess or disturbance this could lead to. Your local Environmental Health Department can advise you on noise reduction measures. Repeated complaints from neighbours will soon give your premises a 'troublesome' name and could easily lead to a formal review of your licence.

Families
Welcoming families into bars can help to create a more civilised style of drinking and a 'family atmosphere'. Premises can now 'opt in' to having children. However, one of the principle objectives of new legislation is to protect children from harm, so you must ensure that your premises are a suitable environment and be able to demonstrate this under the law. This should include standards for acceptable language and behaviour of adults.

Food
Offering food in a bar has the added advantage of providing a way of making money while allowing customers to do something other than drink. Customers who begin by eating are much less likely to get drunk. The availability of food (especially full meals) has been associated with reduced risk of aggression in bars.

Entertainment and games
The type of entertainment you provide is also important in determining the type of customer you're likely to attract. If alcohol is the only 'entertainment', people can drink too much too quickly, which generally leads to problems. However, if the entertainment encourages a lot of competition between customers, this can also lead to problems.

Standing versus seated

Standing areas	Advantages
	• people can dance and move about
	• encourages larger groups
	• creates a social atmosphere.
	Disadvantages
	• more interaction – more opportunity for people to get into arguments
	• large open areas have higher risk of conflict
	• trouble can spread easily.
Seated areas	Advantages
	• tables and chairs act as natural dividers
	• smaller groups, so more manageable
	• factors for conflict are reduced
	• trouble is easier to contain.
	Disadvantages
	• tucked away corners need to be monitored for illegal activities, ie using or dealing drugs.

There is evidence to suggest that providing games such as darts, pool tables or even quizzes will lead to customers drinking more slowly but staying longer. Overall this doesn't mean that customers spend less (evidence suggests that they actually spend more), but because they drink more slowly, they're less likely to become drunk. However, because there is more interaction between people in the games areas, there is an increased likelihood of conflict. Careful monitoring of all areas, especially those where games are played, is essential.

Protective factors versus risk factors

Research carried out in Glasgow in 2005 examined the factors associated with alcohol-related problems in licensed premises, such as drunkenness and violence. The findings were in line with a number of other studies in Canada, the USA, Australia and New Zealand. It found that there is a range of factors that protect against problems in premises and there is a range of factors that increase them. No one factor by itself causes or can eliminate violence, but having a range of the protective factors and making sure there are as few risk factors as possible means the likelihood of problems is much reduced.

Protective factors	• lack of congestion, not overly crowded • inappropriate persons (eg drunk or underage) being refused entry or refused service • good standards of cleanliness and housekeeping • friendly staff • quick and efficient service • calling last orders in plenty of time • managing the exit of patrons • monitoring patrons, including at the entry, the bar and the exit • promotion of food (full meals and snacks) • higher percentage of customers sitting • staff trained in responsible service • good range of reasonably priced soft drinks • good communication between staff.
Risk factors	• unsupervised pool tables • TV showing aggressive, offensive or sexual images or images of intoxication • music that has a lot of offensive words or includes sexually explicit words • congestion anywhere in the premises (at the door, bar, stairs, toilets, dance floor, etc)

- higher percentage of customers standing
- drunk or underage persons allowed in and served
- vomiting
- drug dealing or drug use
- drunk customers in the premises
- staff being hostile or aggressive towards patrons
- staff allowing aggression or watching conflict
- staff sending people outside to fight
- late intervention in situations by staff
- patrons served double at closing time or being served after closing time
- smokiness and/or lack of ventilation
- high level of noise and movement
- lack of bar wiping, table clearing, toilet cleanliness
- openly sexual or sexually competitive activity (such as 'pulling')
- in-house promotion or entertainment focusing on alcohol and 'sexy dancing'.

In summary, premises that have high standards, that are clean and tidy and control the behaviour of their clientele, are more likely to have a good atmosphere and prevent problems.

People skills

Good customer service is only one part of your behaviour. If a situation arises you need to be aware that the way you react will in turn influence the customer's behaviour.

Some people think it's okay to manage a situation using loud threats and even physical force. They allow their own aggression to take over. Most evidence suggests that this is more likely to provoke violence than to prevent it. The police advise that physical force should only be used as a last resort and then only to escort people off the premises.

If you take a loud and overly forceful approach it creates a disturbance and is likely to upset other customers and give a bad impression of your premises. It is much better to try to resolve the problem using good people skills to create a win/win situation – one where the customer leaves without a grievance and the situation has been resolved without threats or violence.

Managing aggression

The table on the next page shows some of the characteristics of three types of behaviour: aggressive, assertive and passive. Ideally you and your staff should aim to be assertive when handling an incident.

It's easy to recognise that people acting in an angry or violent way are being aggressive. Two people, each determined to win an argument, whether or not they obviously become angry, can also be showing aggression. Most people have an aggressive drive. It's very important that the person dealing with an incident – whether it's you or your staff – is aware of their own aggression and able to keep it under control.

What happens when someone gets angry? As the anger grows, the body starts to react physically. You may feel you're losing control, and are likely to show the signs in the 'aggressive' list in the table. This is mainly due to the drug adrenaline. When you are particularly upset or feel threatened, the body reacts in what is known as the 'fight or flight' response. It's getting you ready to stay and fight or run away from danger. If you can remain calm and assertive, you can defuse anger and aggression in others.

Do	• be assertive • be aware of your body language; appear to remain in control • speak slowly and evenly – if you appear calm this will have a calming effect • respect personal space • position yourself where you feel safe, ie behind the counter or stand slightly to one side and not directly facing the other person.
Don't	• get angry – this will increase the risk of conflict • shout or point as this can be seen as aggression • show fear or passiveness.

Removing triggers

Good service can remove some of the 'triggers' that can lead to frustration and anger. Common examples of poor customer service include:
• ignoring customers
• not serving people in turn

Body language

	Aggressive	Assertive	Passive
Posture	Leaning forward, rigid	Upright/straight	Shrinking
Head	Chin jutting out	Firm, not rigid	Head down
Eyes	Strongly focused, staring, often piercing or glaring eye contact	Good regular eye contact	Glancing away or downwards, little eye contact
Face	Set or firm, red (or very white)	Expression fits the words	Smiling even when upset
Voice	Loud, emphatic, speaking quickly, threats	Well modulated to fit content	Hesitant or soft, trailing off at ends of words or sentences, wavering
Arms/hands	Hands on hips, fists, sharp gestures, fingers pointing, jabbing	Relaxed, moving easily, open palms	Aimless, fidgeting
Movement/ walking	Slow and pounding or fast and deliberate	Measured pace suited to the situation	Slow and hesitant or fast and jerky
In general	Heart beating faster, breathing rapidly		

- being rude or unhelpful
- having dirty or messy premises
- leaving stuff lying around and not tidied away – eg empty boxes on shelves in off-sales.

If the outside of the premises advertises an 'upmarket place' then customers will expect a selection of quality wines, beers and spirits and helpful staff who are easily recognisable. However, if what's on offer are cheap brands, staff dressed the same as customers and irresponsible promotions, your customers are more likely to feel frustrated. This can make them become angry, leading to a confrontation with the staff.

Similarly, the service tends to set the tone. Therefore, if different staff treat customers in different ways, or there seem to be different rules for different people, customers will not know what standards are expected of them. This can lead to arguments and conflict between customers and with staff. Research has found that frustration and aggression is more likely if there are different standards, so it's important that there is a consistent standard throughout the premises. This applies to the physical surroundings as well as to the behaviour of staff.

The frustration caused by poor customer service may build up until the customer eventually 'explodes'. The graph on page 93 shows that once someone is already frustrated or annoyed, it won't take much to trigger them into what the graph calls a 'crisis phase'. This could lead to a verbal or even physical assault on you, your staff or other customers.

It's better to try to calm people in the early stages. An example of this would be dealing with a customer complaint immediately and to their satisfaction. If people get to the top of the escalation phase or into the crisis phase, they are much more difficult to control and trouble is more likely.

People may remain in a 'heightened' state for several hours after an aggressive outburst and during this period it is easy to 'trigger' them into repeated outbursts. This is something that servers who are dealing with customers at the end of the evening need to take into account.

Dealing with complaints

A complaint is an opportunity to turn a dissatisfied customer into a satisfied one. It's a fact of life that dissatisfied customers tend to be very vocal. They often tell their friends and family about their bad experience, putting off

The assault cycle

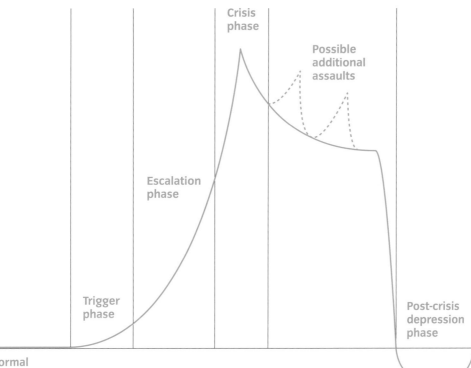

Crisis
phase

Possible
additional
assaults

Escalation
phase

Trigger
phase

Post-crisis
depression
phase

Normal
behaviour

potential customers. Every member of the team should know how to handle complaints, as a badly handled complaint can escalate into an argument or 'verbal conflict'. The dos and don'ts below give the basics.

Do	• listen to the customer without interrupting • try to acknowledge their point of view – you don't have to agree with them, just try to show that you understand, eg 'I can see how that has upset you' • show you're taking the complaint seriously by listening and questioning them to clarify matters • paraphrase or repeat the complaint back to the person: 'So, you're saying that …', which shows you have understood the issue • take action. Tell them what you intend to do, ie pass the complaint to your manager. Better still, write it down.
Don't	• take the complaint personally • let yourself become angry • get into arguments with customers • blame the management or colleagues, which looks unprofessional and shows a weakness in the staff team • try to justify your actions or make complicated excuses – they don't want to know why the problem happened, just what you are going to do about it • make jokes at the customer's expense.
You may need to	• apologise even if it is not your fault, eg 'I'm sorry that there's been a misunderstanding here' • let the customer have the last word.

Audience effect

If you need to 'discipline' someone who has a lot of friends present, this will be very difficult to do in front of the group. The person is likely to 'act up' to his friends to cover up for any 'loss of face'. In this situation it is best to:
• take the person aside so that it's a one-to-one (or get them when they're apart from their friends, such as at the bar or counter)
• avoid making the person look foolish in front of his or her friends

- depersonalise the situation, to focus on the problem of their behaviour and not them personally, eg 'The way you're acting is out of order' is more likely to be tolerated than 'you're an idiot'
- be polite, explain clearly what it is you want them to do (or stop doing) and try to give a reason.

Refusing service

Refusing service is not easy and creates a situation where there's a potential for conflict. How can we refuse service without causing conflict? All of the following tips will help:

- always be polite. It's a good idea to start with an apology, eg 'I'm sorry but…'
- try to give a reason that stresses your legal or professional responsibilities, eg 'It's against the law to serve you without proof of your age. Otherwise I could be fined or lose my job'
- try to follow your refusal with some kind of positive. If this is also a question, it helps to provide a distraction, eg 'Can I get you anything else?'
- be assertive.

Remember you are just refusing service and not rejecting the person!

It's good practice in both on-licence and off-licence premises to keep a refusals book. This is a record of who you have refused to serve and why. The record should give the date and time, plus a brief description of the person refused and the reason for the refusal. It is also useful to note which products the person was attempting to buy. The refusals book shows you are abiding by the laws. It also helps to build a picture of any problem patterns, which will help you address them at an early stage.

Refusing underagers

What would make you suspect that someone is underage? The person may look young, or may be behaving suspiciously, for example, appearing nervous or overconfident. They may be part of a group, with only one coming to the counter or others waiting outside. The type of drinks they're trying to buy may also be an indication, eg high strength ciders, vodka or flavoured alcoholic beverages such as Smirnoff Ice, or products such as Buckfast (fortified wine) and Lambrini (sparkling perry). They may want to buy two half-bottles or pay with lots of small change, or with different batches of money.

As we have learned already, the law says that you must not serve alcohol to anyone under the age of 18. One of the aims of the Licensing (Scotland) Act 2005 is to protect children from harm and as such you are required to operate a 'no proof, no sale' policy. You must not serve anyone who may be under 18 any alcohol unless they produce what is named in the act as 'acceptable proof of age'. If you are still unsure, do not serve them.

Deterring young people

The most effective way of preventing underage sales is to operate in a way that deters young people from attempting to buy alcohol.

- Premises must have a 'Challenge 25' policy in place. This means that every person who appears to be under 25 is asked for proof that he or she is aged 18 or over. All staff need to be vigilant and trained to ask every person who appears to be under 25 for proof of age and must not serve the person unless appropriate proof is shown.
- Display signage informing customers what proof of age will be accepted.
- Regularly review your system, and remind your staff of their responsibilities.

Training them once is not enough! It's also good to test your system by sending in a young mystery shopper. You cannot ask someone who is under 18 to do this, as this would be illegal, but you can use a young-looking 18 year old to test your system.

Tips for off-licence premises

In off-sales premises, groups of young people hanging around and drinking nearby may lead some people to assume that because they're in the vicinity of your premises they are purchasing the alcohol there. To help prevent this you can try to ensure that you distinguish purchases from your shop by:

- having your shop name on price tickets on every product you sell
- using distinctive coloured bags (perhaps showing your shop logo or name).

If there are a number of premises in an area, it can be difficult for the police to track which premises underagers have obtained their alcohol from. In order to help with this, a measure which has been successfully used in a number of areas is colour-coded carrier bags (ie a different colour for each premises) for a period of time in order to track the purchase patterns. Also a common source of alcohol for underagers is their home, or their friends' homes. The use of these bags can help to show that your premises is not supplying the alcohol.

You may also wish to consider:

- installing external security lights, which will normally put youngsters off and move them on to a less well-lit area

· installing CCTV.

It's good practice to ask the group politely to move on, explaining that you have to be especially careful that you are not serving, or appearing to serve, young people. Should this continue to be a problem, you can contact the police, or ask the local authority to apply for an Anti-Social Behaviour Order to prevent individuals acting in this way.

Requesting proof of age

How can you request proof of age without causing conflict?

· Be proactive! Approach the person when they are looking at alcoholic drinks and let them know that proof of age will be required. On-licence premises should speak to the person when they first come in; off-sales should check for proof of age before the person has taken any alcohol or after they have handed it to you for purchase. This reduces the likelihood of theft.

· Make sure that you and your staff are clear and confident about acceptable forms of proof of age. The Licensing Act specifies a passport, a European photocard driving licence, PASS logo or any other document as may be prescribed. Check with your local police which forms of proof of age are acceptable, or discuss this with the LSO, and inform staff so there is no uncertainty.

· Look carefully at the birth date on the proof of age: does it prove that they are over 18?

· Treat the person with some respect. Even if they are underage and cannot buy alcohol, they are still a potential customer for other products and, in the future, for all products.

· Be polite and professional and try not to embarrass the person. Speak to them quietly and evenly, creating as little disturbance as possible.

Test purchasing

Remember also that test purchasing is now legal in Scotland. This is where the police send an underage person (usually a 16 year old) into premises to try to buy alcohol. There is a strict code of conduct governing test purchasing. The underage person is not allowed to try to look older than their age, eg by wearing certain types of clothes or lots of makeup. And they must tell the truth if asked about their age. If you fail a test purchase, ie if you sell them alcohol, then you could be charged, and in such cases licences are commonly suspended for a period of time. If in doubt, don't sell!

Refusing suspected agents

If under-18s cannot purchase alcohol themselves, they will often get a friend or other adult who is 18 or over to buy it for them. This is known as 'acting as an agent' or 'proxy purchase' and is an offence. You have a responsibility to ensure that you do not sell alcohol to an agent.

Signs to look out for (both on- and off-sales):
- if the adult is known or a regular customer and they buy something they don't normally buy or something in addition to their usual order
- a group of young persons gathered outside the shop, or in a quiet corner of the bar or beer garden.

Signs to look out for (off-sales only):
- an adult asking for the same order that has recently been refused to a young person
- an adult asking to pay separately for part of the order (especially high-risk drinks, such as strong ciders, fortified wines or alcopops)
- an adult buying multiples of half or quarter bottles
- an adult making repeat visits in a single evening.

In this situation it is best to:
- politely challenge the person
- explain the legal position, ie that if the drinks are for underage persons, then the server cannot sell them as this would be an offence and the adult would be committing the offence of 'acting as an agent'
- speak to the youngsters and ask them to disperse, or if they're causing a public nuisance, you may wish to call the police and ask them to move the group on.

If the adult denies acting as an agent you may want to:
- watch what the adult does with the drinks
- take the drinks off the under-18s (if it is a bar), and you could also ask them and the adult to leave.

Refusing suspected drunken persons

The law says that you must not serve a drunken person, or knowingly allow your staff to do so. It is also an offence for a drunken person to enter or remain on licensed premises. As we have seen already, it is up to the server to decide if someone is drunk. Most servers agree that if a person is having trouble with their speech or movement, it is likely they are drunk. A person who has been drinking and who is acting in a dangerous or disruptive way could also be classified as drunk.

You may need to approach the person and speak with them to help determine your initial suspicions. This may also give you the chance to detect the smell of alcohol which is often present when a person is drunk. Here is the best practice for refusing service to a drunken person:

- Approach the person ASAP! If possible, meet them at the door and speak with them. If they do come in, it may be more difficult to persuade them to leave.
- Speak slowly and clearly. Remember that the effect of the alcohol on a drunken person will lessen their ability to think and even to understand.
- Keep your voice neutral. Never raise your voice, shout, make loud threats or show any other signs of aggression or anger. This is likely to provoke an angry response in the drunken person and make the situation more difficult to deal with.
- Choose your words carefully. It is better to say something like 'I think you've had (a little) too much to drink', rather than, 'You're drunk'.
- Use the broken record technique. That is, keep repeating the same or similar statements, eg 'I'm sorry, I can't serve you … I could lose my job'.

If you have a well known customer who is regularly drunk, as part of your role as 'friend', it may be helpful if you could speak to them when they come in sober (not when they are drunk), and let them know that you are concerned for their well-being. If their (bad) behaviour is causing you concern, you need to explain the effects that their behaviour is having on you. You also need to explain what changes you require them to make and the consequences (that you will impose) if they don't. You may find it helpful to refer the person to a specialist agency. Alcohol Focus Scotland can provide information on where a person can get help locally.

Closing time (on-licence premises only)

This is the time in the evening when you have to refuse service to everyone. To make matters more difficult, your customers are probably at their most uninhibited (they've had all evening to drink alcohol) and after a long busy evening, you and your staff are probably tired and not at your best. It's not surprising that a lot of incidents happen at this time.

At closing time you shouldn't treat your customers any differently from at any other time. You need to maintain the good relationship that you have built up with them throughout the evening. Remember, if you treat your customers with politeness and respect, that's what you're more likely to get in return. The following closing time dos and don'ts may make for a better day's end.

Do	• have clocks that show the correct time • call last orders in plenty of time • have enough staff to ensure that everyone gets served • when it comes to closing time, make it clear that you're closed, eg switch the bar lights off and leave the bar area • have an established routine that shows you are closed, which may include things such as switching off fruit machines, juke boxes, wine chillers, etc. • clear all glasses, etc., away as soon as they're empty • remind customers quietly and politely as you go around the tables that it is reaching the end of drinking up time • remember to thank customers as they finish their drinks and to wish them good night – you're a host and a salesperson as well, so you want them to come back • chase up stragglers in a friendly manner: 'I hope you've enjoyed your evening, but I have to ask you to finish your drinks now as the bar is closing' • have a proper plan for how people will leave your premises and the surrounding area safely, especially if you have premises that attracts large numbers of people late in the evening. This is sometimes called a 'dispersal policy' (see below).
Don't	• take a 'Jekyll and Hyde' approach to closing time, ie nice one minute, nasty the next. • use loud, unpleasant bells or shouting to signal closing time as this can irritate the customers and set the scene for conflict • serve anyone after the bar has closed as this can lead to accusations of unfairness and arguments • shout at customers or use unpleasant or aggressive tactics as this often makes customers annoyed and more determined to be awkward.

Dispersal policy

If you have attracted a large number of people, you will need to think about how they leave your premises safely and carry on with their homeward journey, especially late at night. Is there more than one exit that they can use to reduce the congestion? Are there ways of encouraging the customers to disperse gradually rather than all leaving at the same time? How can you ensure that the customers leave the area with the minimum noise disruption and other problems? Some premises have stewards outside helping to direct people and calm any trouble spots. Displaying information about the transport services available near to your premises can also be helpful, eg is there a late night bus service and what is its route, taxi information, etc.

See also the closing time checklist in the 'More information' section at the back of this book.

Situations getting out of hand

Occasionally you may face intimidation or aggression from customers. Intimidation can include verbal abuse, racial abuse, threatening behaviour, shoplifting, criminal damage and vandalism. It is important that you and your staff work as a team and everyone keeps a close eye on what's going on. This will help you provide good service and reduce the likelihood of frustration, and also help you prevent situations from getting out of hand.

Stopping trouble early

If you notice that trouble is brewing, you should do something about it. Experienced licensees know that it is much easier to 'nip trouble in the bud' than it is to control trouble that has already broken out. This can be more difficult in off-licence premises as your customers are in the premises for a shorter period of time, giving you less time to identify any problems and decide what action to take.

Monitoring the premises

All parts of the premises should be monitored. In a shop you can monitor customers by using CCTV or mirrors to watch them, or watch them while stacking or tidying shelves.

Customers generally don't like empty shelves in a shop or dirty, cluttered table tops in a bar. If you go about your work with a friendly attitude, people will see your monitoring as good service. This also builds up a good relationship with customers so they're more likely to listen to you if there are problems later.

In a bar or restaurant, it's easy to pass through a crowd and listen to what's going on when you're collecting glasses and wiping down table tops. And if the worst should happen and a fight or a riot (this is rare but has been known to happen) should break out, the other advantage of collecting the glasses should be fairly obvious. Broken glasses or beer bottles can become particularly nasty weapons. If conflict should ever occur at this level, you're advised to get help immediately, preferably from the police by dialling 999.

Danger signals

Depending on what kind of premises you work in, danger signals to look out for can be:

- arguments becoming heated
- raised voices, groups becoming rowdy or silly
- swearing
- individuals playing up to an audience or showing off
- drunkenness
- drinking games or contests (on-licence only)
- large groups gathering together or moving through the premises
- customers looking annoyed
- sudden silence
- regulars behaving out of character
- everyone looking in the same direction
- the sound of breaking glass
- acting suspiciously
- checking for members of staff or security cameras
- groups (or families) splitting up.

Intervention at an early stage

As soon as you become aware of a situation developing, either you or another member of staff should make some kind of intervention. It is important to remember all you have learned about handling aggression:

- keep calm
- don't get angry
- be assertive, not aggressive, and ensure your voice and body language are consistent.

There are several ways to intervene:

Casual intervention	Make your presence known, eg by collecting glasses. This may be enough to quieten things down.
Deliberate intervention	Let people know you've noticed what's going on and that it's not okay! Speak to the persons involved in a calm and assertive way, and always be tactful and polite, using such phrases as 'Is everything okay?' or 'Is there a problem here?'
Distraction	Some skilful servers are able to use distraction as an intervention method – this is easier to do if you know the person a little. You could start a conversation, eg, 'Did you see the football last night?' which can be a distraction from the situation. Alternatively, you could use humour – but you must be careful never to use humour at the customer's expense as this could make the person feel foolish and they may react angrily.

Intervention when trouble has started

Sometimes trouble has got to a very heated stage before you can get there. This makes it much more difficult to take control. In these situations it's best to:

- try to calm and slow things down as much as possible. Remember to speak calmly and slowly and to keep your distance
- try to find out what the problem is. Make sure you listen and, if appropriate, follow the procedure for complaints
- avoid letting other customers get involved, especially if they've been drinking.

You must go through these two steps before you can 'make a request'. When people are in a very heated state, they are unable to think clearly. If you 'make a request', they may not understand what you're asking them to do. Always remember:

1 calm things down
2 REACT – following the steps set out below
3 recognise your own limits.

If you feel that the conflict is getting out of hand (or if you feel it's likely to) get some help from your staff and, if necessary, the police.

REACT is a useful guide for the proper steps to take when dealing with a difficult situation:

REACT	Request Explain Appeal Confirm Take action
Request	The customer is asked to comply with a request, ie tone down their behaviour or leave the premises. If you want someone to do (or stop doing) something in particular, the way you make your request is very important. It is good practice to start with an apology, eg 'I'm sorry, but …' This is polite and makes you seem more approachable and less bossy. If possible, give a reason, eg, 'I'm sorry, but I'm going to have to ask you to keep the noise down a bit. We have to consider the other customers'. Be clear about what you want them to do.
Explain	If the customer doesn't understand the request, or doesn't know why they're being asked to comply with it, you need to provide a clear explanation. They should be told which law or house/store policy they have breached, or what behaviour caused the request.
Appeal	Should the customer still refuse to comply, the request should be repeated and an appeal made to the customer to do what's being asked, eg 'Please stop, I'm sure you don't want to get into trouble with the boss/police, etc.' Explain what action will be taken if they still fail or refuse to comply, eg 'If you keep this up, I won't be able to serve you'.
Confirm	If the customer still refuses to comply with your request, before resorting to the next level of action, you should confirm that the person fully understands what you're asking them to do and that they will not do as asked. Using a phrase

	such as 'Is there anything I can say to you that will make you co-operate?' gives the person one more chance to change his or her mind and comply.
Take action	The final stage, when all other methods of persuasion have failed, is to take action, such as asking them to leave the premises.

Escalation policy

It is good practice to have an escalation policy – a plan of what staff should do and when they should do it if a situation begins to get out of control. Make sure all staff are aware of the premises' escalation policy. In the case of the person refusing to leave the premises, this will usually mean summoning the assistance of other staff or the security staff. Only use physical force as a very last resort and then only to escort someone off the premises. In an emergency situation where your staff or other customers are under threat, you should dial 999 to summon the police immediately.

Drug prevention

As a manager or owner of a premises (licensed or not), under the Misuse of Drugs Act 1971, you cannot knowingly permit drugs such as cannabis and opium to be prepared or used on the premises, since this would be an offence.

But, just as people who are intoxicated with alcohol may be a danger to themselves and others, so those intoxicated by illegal drugs (possibly taken before they entered your premises) may be at risk. You have a social responsibility to do what you can to ensure the health and welfare of all your customers.

Drug-assisted sexual assault (on-licence premises)

There are many reports in the press about 'drink spiking' and 'date rape' drugs, when a person has added something to another person's drink with the intention of committing a sexual assault on them later. Both men and women can be victims of this type of assault; often, the person knows their assailant.

There are a range of drugs used for this purpose, but remember that too much alcohol can produce a similar effect. The effects of the drugs are very

similar to those of excessive alcohol, and can kick in very suddenly. Please be aware that if you or a member of staff think a customer's behaviour has suddenly changed or is out of character for them, this could be the reason.

If a customer tells staff they think their drink has been spiked, staff should take the drink from them and keep it as evidence for the police. Staff should remind customers not to leave their drinks unattended – posters and leaflets are available from the police – and be vigilant for anyone they suspect may be tampering with another person's drink.

Signs of drugs

It's unlikely that you'll actually see any drugs, but there may be tell-tale signs, particularly in such places as the toilets, such as:
- syringes
- pieces of blackened/burned foil, small pieces of wrapped or rolled paper (roaches) or other unusual items
- white powder on surfaces, discarded razor blades
- cut-down plastic bottles with holes punched in them.

Syringes are dangerous. Needles may have blood on them which can carry blood-borne viruses, eg HIV, Hepatitis C. Neither you nor your staff should touch them without taking precautions.
- Use rubber gloves and tongs or tweezers.
- Put the needle into a 'sharp safe' container (available from most drug agencies). If this is not available, use a used drinks can. Insert the needle, sharp end first, into the opening, then tape to seal the can to stop the needle escaping.
- Don't put the needle (or the needle and container) into the rubbish.
- Store it in a safe place until you can ask the advice of your local drugs agency or local Environmental Services Department who may be able to collect it.

Reporting the signs of drug use

It's important to take the signs of drug abuse seriously: staff should know to report anything immediately so you can monitor the signs. They may be an indication of regular drug abuse or dealing on or near your premises (for example, if there is an alleyway nearby).

It's normally appropriate that the police are informed. Any items found should be kept. As with syringes, take care when handling them as they may be

contaminated. It's best if the drugs or paraphernalia, such as bongs, are put into a heavy-duty envelope or container which is sealed and signed by you and a witness, then kept in a safe and secure place until the police can collect it. Collection of the evidence by the police should also be signed for – this procedure may assist with future prosecutions.

Drug dealing

It's difficult to actually establish if someone is drug dealing in an on-licence premises. Drugs are often small and easily hidden – fifty 'street hits' of heroin can be contained in one matchbox!

But people may act in ways that are suspicious. For example, be extra careful if you notice a person sitting in a secluded place, drinking little but staying a long time, especially if:
• they also receive short visits by lots of people
• they use the telephone a lot
• they visit the toilet often
• they make frequent trips outside.

The best gauge of whether a person's actions are 'normal' or not is the experience of you and your staff of what is 'normal' for your customers. Any behaviour that is unusual should be monitored.

If you're suspicious of either drug taking or dealing you must take action. What action you take should be part of your premises' house policy. If you do nothing, you'll develop a problem that will be much more difficult to deal with later. It is very hard to get rid of a bad reputation once it's been established.

It is up to you to look at your premises to assess risks and to minimise the likelihood of problems. If you would like help in assessing your premises' drug risk and identifying the appropriate security measures, your local police and/or drugs agency will usually be able to give advice. The Scottish Drugs Forum or Crew 2000 may also be able to offer help. (For details, see the 'More information' section.)

For more information on drugs (what they look like, the short-term and long-term effects), booklets and leaflets are normally available free of charge from your local health or drugs agency. See www.knowthescore.info for free resources from the Scottish Drugs Forum. *The Facts about Drugs* from NHS Health is a useful resource. Information is also available from police Community Safety Officers.

The police are usually able to arrange a drugs talk/training session (complete with samples and photographs). Often it is the Community Involvement Department that has the responsibility for such talks. This may be an option, particularly if you can arrange to team up with the staff from neighbouring premises to provide a large group for training.

Theft and robbery (off-licence premises)

Unfortunately some people may try to steal alcohol, particularly if they don't think they can get it any other way. There are many measures that can be taken to deter theft, including installing security and surveillance equipment. For advice on this it is best to speak to a qualified expert, such as the police Crime Prevention Officer or a security company.

There are some simple measures that you can take as well:
- always look at and greet people as they enter your premises. This serves two purposes. It welcomes the person to your premises (part of good customer service) and lets them know that you have seen them (sending a message to potential thieves that you are watching!)
- monitor what's going on in your shop, especially around high-risk goods
- be careful with floor displays. Don't arrange or stack goods up too high – it's important that you can see over displays easily
- don't put alcoholic drinks within easy reach of the door. Keep 'high-risk' items, such as high-strength ciders, which can be particularly attractive to young people, in an area where you can monitor them easily.

Shoplifters

Over half of the physical assaults on retail staff are linked to attempted shoplifting. You should ensure staff know what the procedures are in your store if they see a suspected shoplifter. Have a policy. This should make it clear that no-one should risk personal safety to protect property.

Cash

Cash should be kept out of sight and not allowed to build up in the till. Where possible, banking should be done by specialist security staff. It should not be done alone, and should not be done on foot or by public transport. Staff who are expected to do it should be fully trained.

Armed robbery

In the event of an extreme situation such as an armed robbery, the following dos and don'ts sum up advice from professionals.

Do	• exactly what you are told by the robbers • make a mental note to allow you to give a description to police (appearance, details of vehicles, etc.) and listen carefully to identify voices and accents and to pick up the use of names of people or places • keep your distance (if possible) • give loose notes and coins – these will fill a bag more than notes that have been counted and put into neat bundles • inform your superior or line manager as appropriate.
Don't	• show hostility or attempt to fight • argue or speak unless spoken to • try to apprehend or chase the offender away from the store • raise the alarm until it is safe to do so • touch or move anything when the robbers have left – the police may be able to find fingerprints or evidence.

Remember your body language. Keep movement slow and deliberate, as sudden movements may be perceived as a threat and could provoke an aggressive response. The police can provide further advice on how to handle such extreme situations.

Try completing the security checklist in the 'More information' section to see if there are any areas where you could improve.

Barring and excluding customers

When there has been a major incident or when a customer has acted in a reckless or dangerous way, it is tempting to 'bar' the person from your premises. The following dos and don'ts can be a helpful guide:

Do	
	• speak to the person the next time they come in – they will often feel ashamed or sorry for causing the incident and will be much easier to discipline
	• think about what possible action should be taken before speaking to the customer, ie give the person a warning or bar them for a period of time
	• communicate with staff. Tell them what action is being taken. It's important that all staff treat the customer in the same way.

Don't	
	• bar customers 'on the spot'. If the customer is angry and they've been drinking, they will not be thinking clearly. They may feel they have nothing to lose and act in a dangerous or reckless way.

Under the Licensing (Scotland) Act 2005, if the customer was violent you will be able to request an exclusion order (see Part 1).

Best practice following an incident

If an incident has taken place on your premises, whether on-licence or off-licence, you will want to take some steps afterward. Best practice includes keeping an incident diary. This provides a record of all incidents so that causes can be identified and steps taken to prevent problems in future. The entry in the incident diary should give an accurate picture of what happened for purposes of company communication and also for passing on to any authorities that may need details. The diary should be kept in a handy place so everyone knows where to find it. Old ones should be filed for possible use in any legal actions. Be sure to:
• record the incident while it is still fresh in your mind
• note any details that may be required by police or for insurance purposes.

If a crime has been committed, phone the police immediately. Preserve the crime scene while awaiting the arrival of police, and also keep any CCTV evidence.

Reassurance is also important. Recognise that both the customers and the other staff may be anxious. It's best to reassure people that everything is okay and back under control.

Recognise that you've also been through a stressful situation. If possible, take a few minutes to unwind.

Working with others in the community

Pubwatch and Retail Link

Some areas operate Pubwatch schemes where a group of licensees will work together to warn each other about potential problem customers. Groups meet regularly to discuss any issues and often invite a representative from the police to attend.

Retail Link works under similar principles – retailers in an area will work together to warn each other of potential problems, normally shoplifters.

Community Safety Partnership and Safer City Centre

Linking with your local Community Safety Partnership can also be a good way of helping to create better standards in your area. This group is normally police led, and looks at measures to promote community safety. It sometimes has small amounts of funding available for measures that promote community safety. There are similar groups in towns and city centres, often known as Safer City Centre/Safer Town Centre. They normally bring together a number of schemes, such as Pubwatch and Retail Link (sharing information about known criminals, etc) They can cover such diverse things as marshals for taxi queues, responsible drinking messages or Best Bar None schemes.

Liaison with the police

It is good practice to build a working relationship with your local police. This should include reporting any low-level crime or vandalism to allow police to accurately gauge problems in the area and allocate resources accordingly. Deterring these helps to create better standards for your premises and the whole community.

In summary

Training your staff in people skills will help create a friendly environment and bring many benefits for your premises. For example, a server with good people skills will be able to work well as part of a team providing efficient service. He or she will make customers feel noticed and welcome, which will encourage them to come back.

Being able to refuse service to underage persons, drunken persons and those who are trying to buy alcohol for under-18s without giving offence maintains the law and contributes to the good standards of a premises. Efficient service and paying attention to customers prevents attempted theft and potential conflict. Good overall standards and enforcing the law makes your premises more pleasant and safe for staff and customers.

Most conflict can be prevented or controlled by:
- clear signs for the customer that proof of age will be required, and what forms will be acceptable
- friendly efficient service
- good monitoring, both in the premises and in the area outside
- developing a good relationship with the customer
- early intervention if there will be any question about service of alcohol
- removing or reducing any possible sources of frustration
- promoting calmness
- using an assertive, not aggressive, approach.

Finally, in a difficult situation, whether it's refusing service, dealing with a customer complaint, preventing theft or dealing with conflict, don't expect to get it all right the first time. It takes a lot of patience and practice to perfect all the skills.

If you do manage a situation well, remember to give yourself a pat on the back. It's not easy to remain calm and patient. If you don't handle a situation well, don't despair. Try to think about what went wrong, and think about what you could do differently. Try to do better next time.

If you can try to put into practice the things covered in this guide, you will be well on your way to becoming a well-informed and more effective licence holder.

Self check

1 A customer starts shouting at you about having to queue to be served. How would you deal with it?

2 A customer comes into your premises to buy alcohol, but you think they may be underage. What would you do?

3 What would make you suspect that an adult is buying alcohol for an underage person?

4 How would you deal with this?

5 The drinking behaviour triangle shows that three things influencing a person's behaviour. What are they?

6 Why is good customer service important?

7 What is good practice for dealing with conflict?

Test practice

1 Which one of the following should be avoided when dealing with a conflict situation?

a Other staff becoming involved
b Other customers becoming involved
c Asking other staff to help if things seem to be getting out of hand
d Calling the police for help if things seem to be getting out of hand

2 Which one of the following is the appropriate action if staff are being threatened by a customer?

a Phone the local police station
b Phone the LSO to liaise with the police
c Phone off-duty staff to come in and help
d Phone the police on 999

3 Which of the following lists actions that can help to reduce common problems in licensed premises?

1 Acknowledge customers when they enter the premises
2 Ignore customers when they enter the premises
3 Operate a 'no proof, no sale' policy
4 Be aggressive if a customer complains about something
5 Wait until a young-looking customer pays for alcohol before asking them for proof of age

a 1, 2
b 1, 3
c 2, 4
d 2, 5

4 Which of the following best describes how you can keep good standards of behaviour in your premises?

a Be friendly to customers and make it clear what standards you expect of them
b Let those customers who are your friends behave as they want to
c Be friendly to staff and write a list of standards you expect customers to keep to
d Let staff socialise with customers so they think it's a friendly place to be

More information

More information

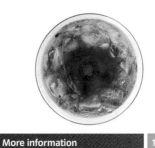

Closing time checklist (on-licence only)

Filling in this checklist could help you see any areas where you could improve.

Name

Date

Name of premises

	Yes	No	Wouldn't work
Do you give clear messages that the bar is closing?	☐	☐	☐
Do you have a consistent routine at closing time, including a music policy, so customers know it is time to leave?	☐	☐	☐
Do you ensure last orders are called early enough to get everyone served?	☐	☐	☐
Do you count down time until closing giving warnings, ie 20 minutes to go, 10 minutes to go, etc?	☐	☐	☐
Do you take all steps possible to show that you are closed, bar lights dimmed, no staff at bar, etc?	☐	☐	☐
Do you ensure that no-one is served after the bar is closed?	☐	☐	☐
Do you and your staff maintain good customer service and remain firm but polite, offering positive remarks, eg 'see you tomorrow'?	☐	☐	☐
Do you have a member of staff at each exit used by customers? This minimises noise and can also ensure that customers don't re-enter. It gives the opportunity to thank customers for coming and wish them good night so they finish their night on a positive note.	☐	☐	☐
Do you give out lollipops or sell burgers? If customers are eating, they can't be shouting.	☐	☐	☐
If there's a cloakroom, is the queue monitored? You may also have extra staff to speed the queue up.	☐	☐	☐
Do you have a dispersal policy to get customers away from the area quickly and quietly?	☐	☐	☐
Do you have one or more 'pavement wardens' in official looking high-visibility jackets outside the premises, requesting people keep the noise down?	☐	☐	☐
Do you empty bottles, etc at a time when it will not disturb neighbours?	☐	☐	☐

Action needed:

Customer service checklist

Filling in this checklist could help you see any areas where you could improve.

Name   Date

Name of premises

Yes	No	
☐	☐	Take a look around with 'fresh eyes' – does the area look tidy, clean, well kept?
☐	☐	How is the overall atmosphere, eg lighting, noise, smell? Is it welcoming?
☐	☐	How well groomed are the staff – are they appropriately dressed and do they look professional?
☐	☐	Are there enough staff on each shift to serve the usual number of customers?
☐	☐	Do you observe staff smiling and greeting customers?
☐	☐	Do you observe staff acknowledging waiting customers when it's busy?
☐	☐	Do you observe staff serving drinks correctly (on-licence only), eg pulling a pint properly, using the correct glasses, handling glasses in line with good hygiene practice?
☐	☐	Is it obvious when staff are on a break and not working?
☐	☐	Do you observe staff being careful with their cash handling and counting the change back to customers?

Action needed:

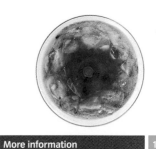

House or Store policy checklist

The Licensing (Scotland) Act 2005 is based on the five licensing objectives and is the law governing the sale of alcohol on licensed premises. As a licence holder you can create a house or store policy that seeks to give guidance to staff on what exactly is and isn't acceptable on your premises to meet – and even exceed – what the law requires. Training can help familiarise staff with what's in your policy and how to use it. The checklist below gives guidance on the areas you may wish to include in an on-licence house policy. There are less options for off-sales, however a store policy should still cover key areas such as the premises details, proof of age, refusing service, drunkenness, staff substance misuse policy and what to do for suspected shoplifters or agents purchasing alcohol for underagers.

1 Premises details

Providing clear details ensures that all staff have access to the correct information. This is particularly important in the event of an emergency or to assist officials, ie, Licensing Standards Officers or police. Have you included the following? Tick if you have included:

- ☐ Name of premises
- ☐ Address and postcode
- ☐ Name of premises licence holder
- ☐ Name of premises manager
- ☐ Name(s) of personal licence holder(s)
- ☐ Telephone number(s)

2 Rules concerning age

Children   Each premises will state in their operating plan if they wish to allow children onto their premises. This plan will form the basis of the premises licence. It is important that staff know what is allowed and what is not, in order that the licence is not breached. The policy might cover:

Are children allowed on the premises?

☐ No   ☐ Yes

If 'yes', tick if you have covered:

☐ At what age are children allowed onto the premises?

House policy checklist continued

☐ At what times are children allowed entry onto the premises?

☐ Which areas of the premises can children enter?

☐ Are there any special requirements? (eg do children have to be accompanied by an adult or there for a specific purpose?) If yes, please list.

Young people The law does allow 16 and 17 year olds to drink alcohol when purchased by an adult with a meal in on-licensed premises; however, you can choose to restrict the sale of alcohol to over-18s only on your premises. Staff need guidance on what is and is not permitted.

Are 16 and 17 year olds allowed to drink alcohol with a meal if it is purchased by an adult on your premises ?

☐ No

☐ Yes

☐ If 'yes', tick if you have covered:

☐ Are staff required to have this sale authorised?

☐ If so, who will authorise the sale,eg premises manager?

Proof of age Although the law allows entry and sale of alcohol to anyone aged 18 or over, you must enforce a '25 policy' whereby staff check the age of all persons who appear to be under 25. Staff need to know what proof of age is acceptable and what procedure they must follow when refusing service, ie entry into refusals book. Tick if you have covered the following:

☐ Who will be asked for proof of age?

☐ What forms of proof of age are acceptable?

☐ What is the procedure for refusing service?

☐ What is the policy for recording refusals, ie is there a refusals book?

3 Drunkenness and public disorder

It is an offence to sell alcohol to a drunken person or to permit a breach of the peace, drunkenness, riotous or disorderly conduct on the premises. Staff must be sure they know what to do, who is responsible and what support is available. Further, staff cannot be drunk on the premises, so not allowing staff to drink or accept drinks protects not only your staff but the licence holder. Tick if you have covered the following:

☐ At what stage will customers be judged as being drunk?

☐ Who will refuse service, ie will the staff inform the personal licence holder or the premises manager who will refuse service? Or will they refuse service themselves?

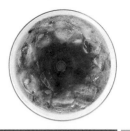

☐ Who will take action in the incidence of disorderly conduct, breach of the peace or riotous behaviour? Will staff inform the personal licence holder, the premises manager or another person, or take action themselves?

☐ What is the policy on drink drivers?

☐ What is the policy on drinking games?

☐ Are staff permitted to drink while on duty?

☐ Can staff accept drinks or tips from customers?

☐ What is the substance misuse policy?

4 Licensed hours

Licensed hours for on-licence premises will be submitted in the operating plan and will form the basis of the premises licence. Off-licence premises will be permitted 10.00 to 22.00, Monday to Sunday. Tick if you have covered the following:

☐ What hours the premises will be open?

☐ What closing time procedures are in place, eg will last orders be called 30 minutes before closing time?

☐ Will the premises be selling off-sales?

☐ If 'yes', what time will alcohol be sold for consumption off the premises?

5 Betting and gaming

Tick if you have covered the following:

☐ Are games permitted on the premises?
  If 'yes':

☐ What games are allowed?

☐ Who will monitor this on the premises?

Other information can also be covered in your house policy, including other possible offences under the Licensing (Scotland) Act and what your policies are to avoid committing them. You may choose to cover other areas such as assisting Licensing Standards Officers, policy on refusal to leave, etc.

Action needed:

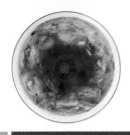

Promoting sensible drinking checklist

Filling in this checklist could help you see any areas where you could improve.

Name | Date

Name of premises

	Yes	No	
			On-licence
	☐	☐	Do you allow anyone to add extra shots to their friends' drinks, eg when a customer says, 'It's her birthday, can you stick another vodka in there'? Customers should always be aware of their own alcohol consumption.
	☐	☐	In groups who are drinking in rounds, do you encourage customers to miss a round if they haven't finished their drink, or to go for a smaller measure?
	☐	☐	Do you have a policy of one drink per person, ie no pints with shots, no double rounds?
	☐	☐	Do you encourage customers to space out their drinks?
	☐	☐	Do you avoid promotions that are time-limited? These tend to make customers feel obliged to try to drink as much as they can in a given period of time.
	☐	☐	Do you avoid promotions that encourage multiple purchases, eg three bottles for the price of two? These tend to make customers drink more than was intended.
			Off-licence
	☐	☐	Do you have information promoting sensible drinking, eg posters or leaflets?
	☐	☐	Do you prevent anyone known to be a problem drinker from purchasing large quantities of alcohol?
	☐	☐	Do you avoid promotions that encourage multiple purchases? These could make customers drink more than was intended.
	☐	☐	Are alcoholic drinks in a separate area of the premises?
	☐	☐	Do you offer alcohol in single serves, eg single cans or bottles?

Action needed:

Security checklist

Filling in this checklist could help you see any areas where you could improve.

Name   Date

Name of premises

	Yes	No
Have you sought specialist advice on the security of your premises from:		
the police Crime Prevention Officer?	☐	☐
the security industry?	☐	☐
the insurance industry?	☐	☐
Do you have procedures for regularly checking that security measures are functioning properly?	☐	☐
Is cash banked daily to keep holdings to a minimum?	☐	☐
Are you complying with your insurance for cash in transit?	☐	☐
Would employees report a theft by a colleague rather than turn a blind eye to it?	☐	☐
Are all staff trained in the procedures for dealing with shoplifters (off-licence only)?		
Do they know who to alert if they are suspicious?	☐	☐
Do they know never to put their own safety at risk?	☐	☐
Do you keep records of all criminal incidents against your business?	☐	☐
If the answer to the question above was 'yes', do you use these records to:		
identify risks that need attention?	☐	☐
monitor the effectiveness of crime prevention measures taken?	☐	☐
quantify how much crime is costing your business?	☐	☐
Is there a system for reporting all incidents of intimidation and violence, including verbal abuse and intimidation as well as physical assaults?	☐	☐
Do staff know what to look for to ensure that credit cards and debit cards are genuine?	☐	☐
Are reports of incidents and security procedures reviewed to see if there is room for improvement?	☐	☐

Checklist continues overleaf

Do you have security measures for the list below?					
Are your staff familiar with them?					
Do they use them regularly?					
Yes	No	Yes	No	Yes	No	
☐	☐	☐	☐	☐	☐	deliveries
☐	☐	☐	☐	☐	☐	doors and windows
☐	☐	☐	☐	☐	☐	stockroom
☐	☐	☐	☐	☐	☐	stock checks
☐	☐	☐	☐	☐	☐	cash handling/forged notes
☐	☐	☐	☐	☐	☐	summoning help
☐	☐	☐	☐	☐	☐	CCTV
☐	☐	☐	☐	☐	☐	locking up/opening up
☐	☐	☐	☐	☐	☐	alarm systems

Action needed:

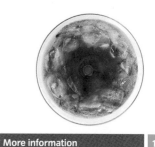

Useful contacts, websites, books and courses

Contacts and websites

Advertising Standards Authority (ASA) is an independent regulator that can provide useful information on advertising and promoting alcohol: www.asa. org.uk, Advertising Standards Authority, Mid City Place, 71 High Holborn, London WC1V 6QT, tel 020 7492 2222, textphone 020 7242 8159, fax 020 7242 3696.

Alcohol Focus Scotland is the Scottish national voluntary organisation for alcohol issues. It provides a range of leaflets, publications and other useful information, including details on where someone with an alcohol problem can get help: www.alcohol-focus-scotland.org.uk, Alcohol Focus Scotland, 2nd Floor, 166 Buchanan Street, Glasgow G1 2LW, tel 0141 572 6700, fax 0141 333 1606, email enquiries@alcohol-focus-scotland.org.uk. Alcohol Focus Scotland also provides a range of training. See ServeWise below.

City & Guilds is a charity established to promote education and training. It is the UK's leading provider of vocational qualifications, offering over 500 qualifications across a wide range of industries. It offers jointly with ServeWise the Certificate for Scottish Personal Licence Holders (Off Sales) and the Certificate for Scottish Licence Holders (On Sales) as well as the Certificate for Staff Working in Scottish Licensed Premises: www.cityandguilds.com, City & Guilds, 1 Giltspur Street, London EC1A 9DD, tel 0844 543 0033, fax 020 7294 2400, learnersupport@cityandguilds.com.

Consumer Direct is a government-funded advice service with regionally based advisors. It can provide advice on the Consumer Protection Act 1987 and other matters: www.consumerdirect.gov.uk, tel 08454 04 05 06.

Crew 2000 provides drugs information and advice for young people: www.crew2000.co.uk, tel 0131 220 3404, email admin@crew2000.org.uk.

Crimestoppers is an independent UK-wide charity working to stop crime: www.crimestoppers-uk.org. You can telephone 0800 555 111 anonymously to report problems.

Drinkaware is a consumer-facing charity promoting responsible drinking. For information about its educational activities, surveys and publications contact: www.drinkaware.co.uk, Drinkaware, Samuel House, 6 St Albans Street, London SW1Y 4SQ, tel 020 7766 9900, fax 020 7504 8217.

Drinkline is an advice and information line for anyone who wants more information about alcohol, local services that can help or simply to talk about drinking and alcohol issues: freephone 0800 7 314 314, www.infoscotland. com/alcohol.

Drugs agency, local. A good source of advice for any drugs-related issues. It may be able to help you assess your premises drugs risk and identify appropriate security measures, or even to collect and safely dispose of needles found on your premises. For more information about drugs go to www.knowthescore.info, tel 0800 587 5879.

Environmental Health Officer at your local council can advise you on matters ranging from the Food Safety Act 1990, to the Smoking, Health and Social Care (Scotland) Act 2005 and noise reduction measures. Also usually in charge of granting Food Hygiene Certificates.

Equality and Human Rights Commission works to eliminate discrimination, reduce inequality and protect human rights. It comprises the two bodies previously known as the Disability Rights Commission and the Equal Opportunities Commission. It provides information to disabled people on their rights and to service providers on their duties under the Disability Discrimination Act 1995. It is also a good source of information on equal opportunities and the Equal Pay Act: www.equalityhumanrights.com, Equality and Human Rights Commission, Optima Building, 58 Robertson Street, Glasgow G2 8DU, tel 0845 604 5510, text 0845 604 5520, fax 0845 604 5530.

Gambling Commission is a regulatory body that can provide information on the Gambling Act 2005 and the Gambling Commission's code of practice: www.gamblingcommission.gov.uk, Gambling Commission, Victoria Square House, Victoria Square, Birmingham B2 4BP, tel 0121 230 6666, fax 0121 230 6720, email info@gamblingcommission.gov.uk.

Health & Safety Executive and Health & Safety Commission publish guides to good practice and offer advice on how to comply with health and safety law. The HSE leaflet Five Steps to Risk Assessment is highly recommended: www.hse.gov.uk, HSE infoline 0845 345 0055.

Licensing Board, local, is one of the main sources of information on the licensing law. They can provide the list of relevant and foreign offences that will be considered for licence applications, mandatory, discretionary and local conditions that apply to your premises, and acceptable forms of proof of age.

Licensing Forum, local, is a statutory body set up to review the operation of licensing law and the local Licensing Board's function in the area. A wide range of interests are represented, including the licensed trade. For more information see www.local-licensing-forums.org.uk.

Licensing (Scotland) Act 2005 and its various accompanying regulations and updates are available to view or print out at www.legislation.gov.uk. You can order a copy from The National Archives, 102 Petty France, London SW1H 9AJ. tel 0870 600 5522.

Licensing Standards Officer (LSO) is an excellent source of information and advice on the licensing legislation and how to ensure that your premises meets all of its responsibilities. The LSO can give advice on the kind of staff training that you should be offering and the records that you should keep, as well as acceptable forms of proof of age, and many other areas. The LSO is normally located in a department of your local council.

Performing Rights Society is the United Kingdom association of composers, songwriters and music publishers. It is a good source of information on music copyright: www.mcps-prs-alliance.co.uk, Copyright House, 29–33 Berners St, London W1T 3AB, tel 0800 068 4828, fax 020 7306 4455.

PRS for Music (formerly Performing Rights Society) is the United Kingdom association of composers, songwriters and music publishers. It is a good source of information on music copyright. www.prsformusic.com, 1 Upper James Street, London W1F 9DE, tel 020 7534 1000, fax 020 7534 1111.

Police, local, can help in many ways. Your police Community Involvement Department can arrange a drugs talk or training session run by a qualified expert. Your local police also may help you identify your premises drugs risk and advise on appropriate security measures. The Crime Prevention Officer can give advice on what you can do to deter theft, low-level crime and vandalism. The police can also put you in touch with Community Safety Partnerships, City Centre Safe groups, and your local Pubwatch or Retail Link.

Portman Group has a code of practice on the naming, packaging and promotion of alcoholic drinks. This code of practice is available on its website or in a printed version: www.portman-group.org.uk, Portman Group, 4th Floor, 20 Conduit Street, London W1S 2XW, tel 020 7290 1460, email info@ portmangroup.org.uk.

Pubwatch is a community-based crime prevention scheme organised by the licensees themselves. National Pubwatch is a voluntary organisation set up to support existing pubwatches and encourage the creation of new pubwatch schemes with the aim of achieving a safer social drinking environment: www.nationalpubwatch.org.uk.

Red Cross (British) offers basic and advanced first aid training at centres throughout the UK: www.redcrossfirstaidtraining.co.uk, British Red Cross Society, Bradbury House, 4 Ohio Avenue, Salford Quays M50 2GT, tel 0844 871 8000, fax 0844 412 2739.

Retail Link is a network of voluntary local groups organised to reduce retail crime by sharing information among themselves and with the local police.

Royal Environmental Health Institute of Scotland promotes the advancement of health, hygiene and safety in Scotland and is a good source of information on food hygiene: www.rehis.org, The Royal Environmental Health Institute of Scotland, 19 Torpichen Street, Edinburgh EH3 8HX, tel 0131 229 2968, fax 0131 228 2926, email contact@rehis.com.

Scottish Drugs Forum is a national non-government drugs policy and information agency. It publishes booklets and leaflets such as *Know the Score*, *Where to Get Help: Directory of Services*, and *Drugs: What Every Parent Should Know*, and can help you, for instance, to assess your drugs risk: www.sdf.org.uk, Scottish Drugs Forum, 91 Mitchell Street, Glasgow G1 3LN, tel 0141 221 1175, fax 0141 248 6414, email enquiries@sdf.org.uk.

Scottish Grocers' Federation (SGF) is the trade association for the Scottish convenience store sector: www.scottishshop.org.uk, SGF, 222/224 Queensferry Road, Edinburgh EH4 2BN, tel 0131 343 3300, fax 0131 343 6147, email info@scottishshop.org.uk.

Scottish Licensed Trade Association represents the interests of all sections of the licensed trade, including pubs, off sales, hotels, restaurants, etc: www.theslta.co.uk, Scottish Licensed Trade Association, Suite 6, 21 Lansdowne Crescent, Edinburgh, EH12 5EH, tel 0131 535 1062, fax 0131 535 1069, email enquiries@theslta.co.uk.

Scottish schools and adolescent lifestyle and substance use survey (SALSUS) was established by the Scottish Executive to provide a broad approach to the monitoring of substance use in the context of other lifestyle, health and social factors. Their website includes reports: www.drugmisuse.isdscotland.org, Substance Misuse Team, ISD Scotland, 1st Floor, Gyle Square, 1 South Gyle Crescent, Edinburgh EH12 9EB , tel 0131 275 7777.

Security Industry Authority (SIA) manages the licensing of the private security industry as set out in the Private Security Industry Act 2001. It also aims to raise standards of professionalism and skills within the private security industry: www.sia.homeoffice.gov.uk, Security Industry Authority, PO Box 1293, Liverpool L69 1AX, tel 0844 892 1025, fax 0844 892 0975.

ServeWise is the training arm of Alcohol Focus Scotland, providing training to people working at all levels within the licensed trade in Scotland. All ServeWise courses meet the necessary legislative requirements. ServeWise offers trainer training for qualifications such as the Certificate for Scottish Personal Licence Holders and the Certificate for Staff Working in Scottish Licensed Premises. It also offers training for licensing officials such as LSOs and Licensing Board members. See www.servewise.co.uk, tel 0141 572 6703, email servewise@alcohol-focus-scotland.org.uk

Smoke Free Scotland provides information and guidance on smoking legislation: www.clearingtheairscotland.com.

St Andrew's Ambulance Association offers first aid training ranging from two hours' tuition on basic resuscitation skills to week-long courses for first aiders in the workplace: www.firstaid.org.uk, St Andrew's Ambulance Association, St Andrew's House, 48 Milton Street, Glasgow G4 0HR, tel 0141 332 4031, fax 0141 332 6582.

Trading Standards Officer, local, can provide more information about requirements under the Weights and Measures and Trades Description Acts.

Useful books

Conflict Management in the Workplace, City & Guilds and Maybo, offers excellent advice for managing conflict. To obtain copies email learningmaterials@cityandguilds.com or tel 020 7294 4113.

ServeWise Refusals Book offers information and prompts to staff on the law regarding the refusal of service as well as giving staff the opportunity to record details of refusals with useful tear-out cards that can be given to customers who are being refused service. To obtain copies email servewise@alcohol-focus-scotland.org.uk or tel 0141 572 6703.

Workbook for Staff of Licensed Premises, ServeWise and City & Guilds, an excellent resource to use to record staff training. To obtain copies email learningmaterials@cityandguilds.com or tel 0844 543 0000.

Relevant courses

Certificate for Scottish Personal Licence Holders (On Sales) 7104-01, City & Guilds and ServeWise

Certificate for Scottish Personal Licence Holders (Off Sales) 7104-02, City & Guilds and ServeWise

Certificate for Staff Working in Scottish Licensed Premises 7104-03, City & Guilds and ServeWise

Conflict Management 1884, City & Guilds

Door Supervision 1900, City & Guilds

First Aid Offered by both the British Red Cross and St Andrew's Ambulance Association (contact details above)

Hospitality and Catering City & Guilds and HAB offer a range of qualifications from entry level to advanced on all aspects of hospitality and catering

Licensing Board Members Training ServeWise

Licensing Standards Officers Training ServeWise

Security Guarding 1902 City & Guilds

Trainers' Qualification ServeWise

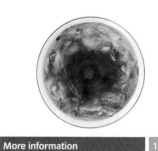
Test practice answer key

1 Licensing law (page 33)	1 c, 2 a, 3 a, 4 b, 5 c, 6 b, 7 b
2 Other key legislation (page 51)	1 a, 2 c, 3 b, 4 a
3 Alcohol – and its influences (page 78)	1 a, 2 b, 3 c, 4 c
4 The premises environment (page 114)	1 b, 2 d, 3 b, 4 a

Illustrations

City & Guilds would like to acknowledge the following:
· iStock (www.istockphoto.com) pages 7 above Sean Locke, below Lise Gagne; 10 gprentice; 11 above Sharon Dominick, middle Lise Gagne, below Valerie Loiseleux; 14 ranplett; 15 above Nick Free, below Michael Walker; 26 Nick Free; 27 above Bob Thomas; 37 above Jacob Wackerhausen, below ilbusca; 41 Achim Prill; 42 stocksnapper; 43 Claudio Baldini; 44 Ivan Mateev; 48 above Robert Kohlhuber, below Sergei Sverdelov; 49 Matthew Scherf, 55 above and below Lise Gagne; 57 Eric Gevaert; 59 above Bob Thomas, below Lise Gagne; 64 Ljupco; 70 Floortje; 71 above naphtalina, below Rebecca Ellis; 81 above Lise Gagne, below Sean Locke; 84 Steve Diddle; 85 above Sharon Dominick; 86 above Mustafa Deliormanli, below Melanie Kintz; 88 above Jacob Wackerhausen, below Simon Podgorsek; 89 above Xavi Arnau, below Paul Vasarhelyi; 96 above ilbusca; 97 Michael Walker; 108 above Christopher Steer; 109 Martin Lladó
· Jane Smith pages 56, 75
· Max Ackermann pages 40, 85 below
· ServeWise pages 27 below, 96 below, 108 below